241.6765
E48n

W9-ADK-490

No-Nonsense Dating

WILDER BRANCH LIBRARY
7140 E. SEVEN MILE RD.
DETROIT, MI 48234

Ronn Elmore, Psy.D.

HARVEST HOUSE PUBLISHERS

EUGENE, OREGON

2008
JUL · WI

Unless otherwise indicated, all Scripture quotations are taken from the New King James Version. Copyright ©1982 by Thomas Nelson, Inc. Used by permission. All rights reserved.

Verses marked NIV are taken from the HOLY BIBLE, NEW INTERNATIONAL VERSION®. NIV®. Copyright©1973, 1978, 1984 by the International Bible Society. Used by permission of Zondervan. All rights reserved.

Verses marked NASB are taken from the New American Standard Bible®, © 1960, 1962, 1963, 1968, 1971, 1972, 1973, 1975, 1977, 1995 by The Lockman Foundation. Used by permission. (www .Lockman.org)

Verses marked NCV are taken from *The Holy Bible, New Century Version,* Copyright © 1987, 1988, 1991 by Word Publishing, Nashville, TN 37214. Used by permission.

Verses marked MSG are taken from The Message. Copyright © by Eugene H. Peterson 1993, 1994, 1995, 1996, 2000, 2001, 2002. Used by permission of NavPress Publishing Group.

Verses marked NLT are taken from the *Holy Bible,* New Living Translation, copyright ©1996. Used by permission of Tyndale House Publishers, Inc., Wheaton, IL 60189 USA. All rights reserved.

Verses marked HCSB are taken from the Holman Christian Standard Bible®, Copyright © 1999, 2000, 2002, 2003 by Holman Bible Publishers. Used by permission. Holman Christian Standard Bible®, Holman CSB®, and HCSB® are federally registered trademarks of Holman Bible Publishers.

Cover by Koechel Peterson & Associates, Inc., Minneapolis, MN

NO-NONSENSE DATING
Copyright © 2008 by Dr. Ronn Elmore
Published by Harvest House Publishers
Eugene, Oregon 97402
www.harvesthousepublishers.com

Library of Congress Cataloging-in-Publication Data

Elmore, Ronn.
No-nonsense dating / Ronn Elmore.
   p. cm.
ISBN-13: 978-0-7369-2347-7
ISBN-10: 0-7369-2347-0
1. Single people—Conduct of life. 2. Dating (Social customs)—Religious aspects—Christianity.
3. Marriage—Religious aspects—Christianity. I. Title.
BV4596.S5E46 2008
241'.6765—dc22

2008002129

All rights reserved. No part of this publication may be reproduced, stored in a retrieval system, or transmitted in any form or by any means—electronic, mechanical, digital, photocopy, recording, or any other—except for brief quotations in printed reviews, without the prior permission of the publisher.

Printed in the United States of America

08 09 10 11 12 13 14 15 16 /VP-NI/ 10 9 8 7 6 5 4 3 2 1

To my sweet, strong Abba,
whose perfect love truly does cast out fear.

Acknowledgments

If a man's wealth could be measured by the extraordinary love and support that surround him, I am truly rich. Among the treasures in my portfolio are:

Angela DePriest is equal parts agent and cheerleader. Her get-it-done attitude and gifted pen helped me bring this book to life.

Terry Glaspey and **Nick Harrison** are proof positive that editors really can be all about the book and the business and be honorable gentlemen at the same time.

Rob Cummings not only makes The Ronn Elmore Group operate smoothly, he keeps me from getting distracted so that I can think, write, and speak with focus and genuine joy.

Jeff Herron and **Melvyn Barney** have made praying with me and for me their unceasing priority. I'm amazed by their sincere devotion to God—and to me.

My incredible wife, **Aladrian**, is stunning evidence that God does exceedingly abundantly beyond whatever I could have asked or thought. I still can't believe I get to be loved by her every day.

Contents

A Prayer for Knowledge and Discernment

The theme of *No-Nonsense Dating* is also my prayer for you. You'll find it in Philippians 1:9:

> *And this I pray, that your love may abound still more*
> *and more in knowledge and all discernment.*

I'm starting with the assumption that you already have some love in you. Maybe you've been in love before...or maybe you haven't. Either way, I'm going to also assume that you desire to enter into an enduring relationship (that may even include marriage) before Jesus comes back or before you breathe your last breath; and that the love God put in you will end up with someone somewhere, for better or for worse, for a little time or for a long time.

So my prayer is not that you simply find the mate of your dreams, but that you find abounding love that is well-balanced, deliberate, and characterized by action that benefits your partner without discounting yourself—love that results in actions that are sensitive, creative, and meaningful without being self-devaluing, manipulative, or excessively self-protective. I pray that you find real satisfaction in your love life; the abiding contentment and confidence that comes from committing to love someone, feeling loved in return, and knowing and doing the actions that effectively demonstrate your love.

My prayer is not that you simply get some love, or that you will be able to avoid the wrong people who will not take care of the love you offer. My prayer is exactly what the apostle Paul's prayer was for the people of Philippi—that the love inside you will overflow with some *new* stuff, with even more knowledge and discernment.

The Power to Make Decisions

When Paul uses the word "knowledge" in Philippians 1:9, he is basically talking about what we might call "book wisdom." It's just technical intelligence, like two plus two equals four. Paul says he wants you to have an intelligent kind of love, not the kind where you fall in love and lose your mind and emotions. You don't want to go wherever your heart leads you. That's dangerous. You want to go where your heart leads you only if your head has already signed off on the idea. That's loving wisely.

Discernment is a little different from knowledge. The first part of that word ("dis") is akin to the Latin word "duo" meaning two. A diametric opposition means somebody is on one side and somebody else is on the other side. Discernment literally means good judgment—being able to tell the difference between two or more good-looking things. Discernment comes from practicing good judgment.

The fewer relationship experiences you've had in the past, the more you are likely to think, *How difficult can it be to meet the right person?* But if you've been involved in a few romantic relationships only to see them sour, you *know* firsthand how hard finding the right person can be.

It would be easy if all you had to do was choose between a low-down person and a wonderful person. But that's not how it usually works. Instead, you're out there having to choose between two (or more) wonderful-looking opportunities for love. The problem is that nobody looks or acts like a dog the first time you meet—even a dog knows how to *not* look like a dog when he (or she) puts himself (or herself) on the market!

No relationship looks sick at first. It looks rewarding, healthy, and even like a blessing from God. You know how it is. You have friends who call you and say, "Girl, I have met *the one.* My middle name starts with *L* and his middle name starts with *L.* And when we went out to lunch together, we both wore blue jeans. God is all over this." Or your friend will say, "Her favorite movie is *Scarface* and my favorite movie is *Scarface.* Her favorite color is yellow and my favorite color is yellow. God has put us together."

Some of you may be rolling your eyes and laughing, but this kind of thing happens every day. Those of you who know people like this may be laughing too—but for a different reason. Because what happens next? A week or two passes and when you ask your friend how the God-ordained relationship is going, you hear about how low-down, awful, sick, defective, dysfunctional, and pathological the other person is! Like I said, a little discernment goes a long way.

The senses that help you distinguish good from bad must be developed, sharpened, and trained by those who have experience. You are a wise person if you seek counsel with trained individuals and learn from them. That's why I'm so glad you chose this book. I've dedicated my life's work to teaching people just like you how to sharpen your discernment skills so you can take them into the world and use them in real situations and real relationships.

A Few Simple Rules

Experienced, mature people know that there are two kinds of rules—rules from books that contain knowledge and rules from training where you learn to read between the lines. You'll need both kinds to evaluate yourself and a potential mate.

> *Love is like playing the piano. First you must learn to play by the rules, then you must forget the rules and play from your heart.*
>
> UNKNOWN

I know—all your life you've heard that rules are in place to protect you, and yes, that holds true in relationships too. Whether you're putting yourself out there for the first time, or you're a seasoned veteran at pitching woo, there are rules to developing an intelligent kind of love. Break those rules and someone gets hurt. If you've ever been badly hurt in a relationship (and most of us have), then you know what I'm talking about. You've probably said, "If I ever get into another relationship, I'll *never* handle it like that again. I'll *never* break that rule again."

So as you read this book, learn the few simple rules and put these suggestions into action. Just remember what Paul says: "I pray that your love may abound still more and more in knowledge and discernment." That is my utmost prayer for you on the way to the one for you.

Dr. Ronn Elmore

Introduction

Gravitation is not responsible for people falling in love.

ALBERT EINSTEIN

⚬≺

Making the decision to date is tough. The act of dating is even tougher. So before you just throw yourself out there, let's spend some time talking about your goals and priorities as they relate to dating.

Obviously, one primary goal is learning how to recognize your soul mate—*the one*—when he or she comes along. But an even more important priority is keeping your relationship with the Lord in focus. After all, your relationship with the Father is the most important relationship you'll ever have. All other relationships in your life will be a mere reflection of your relationship with Him.

We're also going to confirm or dispel certain myths about dating that have been thwarting Cupid's efforts for many years. In certain circles dating has received a bad rap for a long time, and it's high time you knew the truth. I'll redefine the concept of dating and you'll begin to see that the dating process is a positive step you need to take to reach certain relationship goals in your life. This is true whether you're a man or a woman.

Dating Preparation for Singles

Everything you'll learn in this book is designed to help you move down the path toward finding *the one*—experiencing and learning all the inward and outward lessons that you, as a single adult, must assimilate on the way to the love of your life. After years of experience in the field of relationships and dating, I'm confident this is a plan that works well when followed diligently.

Let's take a quick look at what you'll find in each of the chapters in this book.

1. Dating Myths Derailed
There are plenty of misconceptions about dating. You'll find out what dating is—and what it isn't.

2. Vive la Différence!
You'll learn to appreciate—even celebrate!—the differences in how men and women communicate and behave, and avoid getting stuck in semantics or bogged down in unintentional misunderstandings.

3. Define What You Want
You'll learn to maximize your time during your season of singleness and clarify your tastes by identifying the unique type of mate you will be and the unique type of mate that suits you.

4. The Product Is You!
You'll learn to increase your relationship success by presenting "Your Very Best You" for optimum exposure and advantage, and to reinvent yourself each time the need arises.

5. Market Yourself
You'll learn the importance of having a plan—so the world will see and interpret the product (you) in the best possible light.

6. Show Up—And Get in the Game
You'll find out the very best places to go in order to meet the kind of quality person with whom you want to spend your time.

7. Approach and Be Approachable
You'll find out the importance of staying focused and goal-oriented

by learning the detailed, practical strategies of moving from "first sighting" to the introductory and evaluation stages and on to a committed relationship and possibly marriage.

8. Reveal Yourself—And Be Real
You'll shed your excess baggage so you can discover and replace the hidden thought patterns that may have sabotaged your past relationship efforts.

9. Balance Your Love Life with Your Whole Life
You'll discover the importance of having a balanced life filled with family, love, work, and worship. You really *can* have it all.

10. Make Decisions
You'll learn there are things you can do, things you should do, and even things you shouldn't do, when looking for a mate.

As you start reading this book, you'll find that it's not just a book you read and then put down when you reach the last page. If you've read any of my other books (of course, I recommend that you do!), or if you've heard me speak, you know I'm a man of action. This book, like all my other books, is not just a "think about it" book. It's a "do something about it" book. *The best advice is only truly effective when it's lived and not just learned.*

So grab your favorite Bible and let's get started, shall we?

CHAPTER ONE

When the World Was Flat

Most of us were indoctrinated into a magical, mythical culture when our parents told us about the Easter Bunny and the Tooth Fairy. I remember putting a tooth under my pillow and trying to stay awake to catch a glimpse of the elusive Tooth Fairy. I never caught him (or her?), but my belief in the myth was reinforced every time I found a shiny nickel under my pillow.

We were also told as children that Santa Claus would bring nice presents to good little boys and girls, so we tried our level best to have spiffy table manners, always say "please" and "thank you," and not push our little brothers down the stairs.

How did our beliefs in myths alter the way we behaved? Didn't we all feel just a little silly when we found out the myths weren't real? How many of us are going to pass on these time-tested myths to our own children?

We're taught myths because, in part, someone in authority over us wants us to behave in a certain way. It's fun for them, and most of the time it's good for us.

But there have been other myths that weren't so innocent, and they weren't created to control our behavior, although they certainly had a huge impact on how we behaved. For instance, before the age of exploration everyone believed the world was flat. After all, you could see the line of the horizon in the distance. Sailors and explorers feared that if they traveled to that point on the horizon, they would fall off the edge of the earth! People of that era believed what they were told because there was no disputing evidence. It took the likes of Pythagoras and Aristotle to convince everyone that the earth was spherical in form. And it wasn't until the fifteenth century that Portuguese explorers like Magellan removed all doubt about the myth of a flat world.

Even today we are all easily led by unsubstantiated rumors, the latest studies, advertisements, and even hearsay! There are so many things we believe that defy rational explanation; what we believe as truth influences how we behave and how we make decisions.

There comes a time, though, when childish myths must be revealed and the real truth must be told. As adults we can't live our lives under the misguided impression that Santa Claus will bring us presents if we are good or that the Easter Bunny will bring us candy if we volunteer at the local shelter.

Santa Claus is a myth. The Easter Bunny is a myth. The Tooth Fairy is a myth. And the world is not flat. It's easy to be distracted from the truth about important life issues when you're afraid you're going to fall off a ledge into some dark abyss. Learning the truth sets you free to pursue your dreams without fear. Isn't it time to dispel some myths about dating?

1

Dating Myths Derailed

You will have some false teachers in your group.
They will...teach things that are wrong—
teachings that will cause people to be lost.

2 PETER 2:1 NCV

For some of you, it may be hard to accept the fact that there are no magical solutions to your drooping, sagging, or nonexistent love life. But if you can move beyond unrealistic expectations of magical solutions, you can learn to move ahead in your love life by learning to make wise decisions. And that's what we'll be talking about throughout the book—making the right decisions that will advance your relational life.

Wise decision making starts with learning the truth about what dating really is and how it fits into a balanced life. You must also be willing to abide by certain relational rules or principles.

So in an effort to learn what dating is and how it fits into your life, let's consider some of the most common dating myths, expose them for what they are, and put them back into a context you can use. To do this, let's look at some of the questions I'm commonly asked about dating.

James, age 26, from Omaha says:
> Dr. Ronn, I'm a Christian, and I think dating is pointless unless it works toward a "purpose." I don't want to be wasting my time unless I know the woman I date is going to be the woman I marry.

MYTH #1: *Dating is pointless unless it has a specific purpose—namely marriage.*

James, you say you want dating to be serious, working toward a "purpose." Frankly, that attitude makes you sound as if you're too good, as if you're holding yourself to a higher standard—one very few people can attain. (And therefore you're still single. Hmm.)

When two Christians who really don't want to *date* but would rather work toward a permanent relationship get together, it puts a tremendous, almost insurmountable, strain on a first date (or a second, third, or tenth date). Talk about a failure to meet expectations! Face it, sometimes going out to the movies with another person is just that...not some meaningful step on the way to Christian marriage. This enormous pressure is, in my opinion, counterproductive to the long-range goal of a permanent relationship.

This is a perfect book for you, James, because the message is this: If you want to date only with a purpose, then date with a purpose. But let's dispel the myth that all dating is pointless unless it has that specific purpose. Don't take dating too seriously. Just get out there and have some fun!

Shanti, age 28, from Los Angeles says:

I have lots of guy friends who are really great! But I would never date them because they're my friends.

MYTH #2: *You should never date your friends.*

Dating can sometimes be about nothing more than simple companionship and the building of friendships. I happen to be one of those people who think men and women *can* be friends! Dating is a way to have fun, get out, and be seen by a greater number of potential mates—after all, it's all in the numbers! It's also a great way to learn about yourself.

Shanti, if you have male friends who have all the qualities you're looking for in a potential mate, why not date one of them? I would think that someday you'd want to have a husband you can laugh and have fun with for the rest of your lives. Some of the most successful marriages I've seen began as a friendship. Those long-term relationships are sustained by this simple statement: He (or she) is still my best friend!

Successful dating doesn't include any hard and fast rules about dating friends, but this business about *not* dating a friend is just a myth. In 1994 a book called *Sex in America: A Definitive Survey* revealed that 63 percent of married couples met through friendships.[1] More than a decade later, that figure hasn't changed significantly.

If there is a mutual, healthy, and respectful attraction, start there. Work toward a dating relationship that includes large doses of open communication, and just see where it leads. The key is in respecting each other enough as friends to stay on the same page as the relationship progresses toward something more substantial or remains just a great friendship.

Ruth, age 28, from Chicago says:

> Dr. Ronn, I've never really dated, I don't have a lot of experience with the opposite sex, and I'm not willing to kiss a lot of frogs, if you know what I mean. So I think I'd rather just wait until *the one* comes along and finds me.

MYTH #3: *You have to kiss a lot of frogs to find a prince.*

There is an interesting myth hiding in this statement, Ruth. The myth is *not* in the fact that you have to kiss a lot of frogs. (Life is all about kissing frogs. It's unavoidable.) The myth is that finding a prince is the reward for all the suffering involved in frog-kissing. Unless you're just in the market for a prince, the fun dating experience should be its own reward!

The dating experience is just like a day on the beach, being in the water, enjoying the sun and the moonlight, feeling the sand between your toes. Would you pass all that up just because you've never vacationed in the islands? "Well," you might say, "I've never been to a beach, so I think I'll just stay home and wait for someone to send me a little vial of sand from the islands." No! You plan carefully, pack your suitcase, make your reservations, and you go and enjoy the experience. The beach will not come to you, Ruth.

While you're out and about, you're gaining dating experience, and learning about the opposite sex and human relationships. Your goal is to gain enough experience to recognize *the one* when he comes along—the different-ness and the right-ness of that man.

Dive in, Ruth, the water is fine!

Marcus, age 30, from San Antonio says:
> The last woman I asked out on a date turned me down flat and told me she wasn't interested in men who want to "try out the merchandise." Dr. Ronn, what exactly did she mean by that? And is that what I'm doing when I go on a date?

MYTH #4: *Dating is nothing more than "trying out the merchandise."*

"Trying out the merchandise" is a rather crude way to put it, Marcus; however, I personally think this is a *huge* reason to date! I mean, you do find a lot of great apples when you're shopping for apples, right? And you'd never dream of investing a grand sum of money into a new car without doing your homework, shopping, and comparing, would you?

One of my goals in writing this book is to offer a great resource for women and men who have the negative opinion that dating is nothing more than "getting the milk for free." In a healthy and respectful,

God-honoring dating relationship, two people share a mutually satisfying bond—they have both decided to die to self and give the other
person what he or she needs.

Marcus, this woman was telling you that she didn't trust you to
take care of her heart, and that's the sign of a deeply wounded person.
She is in need of understanding on your part and true healing and
comfort from God. But in a healthy dating relationship, you're not
"trying on the merchandise," you're both trying on your future to see
how it fits. That's a good and wise thing to do.

Julia, age 32, from Denver says:

Here is the bottom line for me, Dr. Ronn. I was taught that I
cannot "market" myself as a single Christian woman. Proverbs
18:22 makes it clear that I'm supposed to wait for him to find
me, right?

MYTH #5: *Proverbs 18:22 says women should not initiate dating rela-*
tionships.

Au contraire, Julia! Let's dispel this myth once and for all. So before
you read any further, let me say this: The Bible is never wrong. It
never lies. It never deceives. However, plenty of well-meaning men
and women have misinterpreted many things in the Bible in an effort
to "protect" young people.

Julia, nowhere in the Bible will you find the name of your mate. The
Scriptures do guide us in matters of the heart, and God has laid down
certain rules we must follow before we can choose from the gifts He
gives us. But the idea that Proverbs 18:22 claims women can't pursue
romantic relationships is pure myth. The Scripture reads: "He who
finds a wife finds a good thing." That doesn't mean *he* is the only one
that should be working on the relationship. It only means that when
a man marries, God is happy about it.

I don't want to appear irreverent, but there is nothing wrong with men *and* women committing to some sound, honest, biblically based relationship marketing. There's nothing wrong with reading books about dating and relationships, and there's nothing wrong with a woman letting a man know that she is available and interested. Don't fall into the Proverbs 18:22 trap. Be wise in all matters.

Georgia, age 36, from Boston says:

> If it's all statistics, then the majority of single men I meet will be losers! My single friends keep telling me that men are like parking places—all the good ones are taken and the rest are handicapped!

MYTH #6: *People are single because there is something very wrong with them, and most of those people will end up on the other side of your restaurant table.*

Let's face it, Georgia—the world is a big place, and there are a lot of wonderful men and women in it. But there are also a lot of fools, some crazies, and some dogs too. It's true! It's just statistics! In fact, there are nearly 98 million single people out there![2] You can't conclude that everybody you meet will be a fool, a crazy, or a dog. There are a lot of good folks out there whose lives are fascinating and whose walk with God is seasoned and mature.

This book will be a great guide for helping you navigate around that sliver of the unmanageable, undateable population. Knowing yourself is the first step to knowing what to look for in another person. Slow down, take your time, get to know yourself a little better, and get to know what you're looking for in another person before you jump into the relationship market. Knowledge and discernment are lessons you'll learn here, and those things will help you beat the odds and deal with the fools and the crazies along the journey. Honestly, most single people aren't single because there is something "very wrong" with them. Like you, they may be single because they have very high standards and expectations.

One more thing, take your friends' advice with a grain of salt and look at their advice in the context of their lives and their own painful experiences. Make sure they're speaking the truth with love and with your best interests at heart before you set them up as an expert about *you*.

Malcolm, age 40, from Philadelphia says:

> Dr. Ronn, I've been dating the same woman for six months now, and we're committed to waiting until our wedding night. Some of my friends tease me about this, and I'm beginning to wonder if waiting is an outdated rule. What do you think?

Myth #7: *Consummating your life together on your wedding night is old-fashioned, and no one follows that old rule anymore.*

Sorry, Malcolm! As much as those people want to try to convince you that waiting until the wedding night is old-fashioned, I think that they are only trying to convince themselves so they can justify their own behavior. If you read the Bible and you want to follow God's will for your life, then you'll do what He says: *Wait!*

And what is wrong with "old-fashioned" anyway? Depending on how long they lived, our grandparents and great-grandparents celebrated fiftieth, sixtieth, and seventieth wedding anniversaries! Six months is not a long time to spend getting to know one woman, and finding out if she is the one with whom you want to spend the rest of your life. Wisely, you have both committed yourselves to waiting until you're married, and you should stick to that plan. It's a good one. Spend this time knitting your souls together based on everything *except* sex. When the time arrives for you to introduce sex to your married relationship, you'll both know you're not together for purely physical reasons.

Honor God and each other, Malcolm. Hold fast to your commitment and stand up to your friends when they try to apply the pressure to conform to their standards of behavior.

Shelvy, age 38, from Houston says:

There is this guy who browses a lot at the bookstore where I work, and I am very interested in him. But I'm never going to have a body like Tyra Banks, and that's what all the guys are looking for.

MYTH #8: *Only the thin, rich, beautiful people get all the bona fide dates.*

Well, Shelvy, I guess it doesn't hurt to be thin, rich, or beautiful. But I know a lot of thin, rich, and beautiful people who are very unhappy in their relationships and in their lives in general. First of all, to assume that all guys are looking for the next top model or movie star would mean that all guys are shallow, and that just isn't so. According to a TopDatingTips.com poll, only 11 percent of respondents say looks are the most important thing about a person, whereas 30 percent say personality is more important than looks. Yes, it's true that 67 percent say looks do matter, but only 30 percent of those people say that's the *first* thing they notice. Eyes and personality rank second in what people notice first about someone they're interested in dating.[3] Another poll shows 69 percent of respondents say looks are important but *not* as important as personality![4] So maybe it's true that looks do matter—at first glance. But when it comes down to choosing a partner, a man will look beyond what he sees. He'll look for something in a woman that makes him feel special.

Understand that dating, in essence, is a numbers game—especially to men. What I mean is that a man will show up in places where he thinks he has a chance. He may talk to ten women and get turned down flat by seven of them. Two may show some mild interest, and one may flash him a smile that says, "I'm *the one!*" He'll pursue the one who opens the door to his heart and makes a way for him to do his thing, even if she doesn't look like Tyra Banks. Try putting yourself in front of him and flashing your beautiful smile. I can't promise you'll be given an engagement ring in 30 days or less, but you'll be a bolder and more confident woman for it, and you never know who else might see that smile of yours.

Tisha, age 32, from St. Louis says:
> Dr. Ronn, all my girlfriends say I'm better-off single, lonely, and not dating at all. All my male friends say I'm better-off having something to do on Friday nights. So which is it?

MYTH #9: *It is better to be single, lonely, and not dating anyone than attached and miserable.*

Oh, Tisha, what you'll hear in nearly every testosterone-laden locker room in America is that it is better to be attached, discontented, and having regular sex than to be single and having no sex at all. If relationships were *only* about sex, then that might be true. But let me suggest a new idea to you: You don't have to be "single, lonely, and not dating anyone" *or* "attached and miserable." Both options imply feelings of complete and utter despair and discontent! You don't want that! Tisha, you can be single, dating, and happy or committed (maybe even married) and happy. The reason why you date is to find the one that is perfect for you. The time spent dating is supposed to be a fun and adventurous experience. Don't let other people bring you down with talk of being lonely and unhappy. Use your season of singleness to create happy memories for yourself—memories that include only you, memories of experiences with your friends, and memories of your dating experiences. Kick despair and discontent to the curb! And if your friends keep bringing you down with all their "well, you're just better-off" talk, then kick them to the curb too! You need friends who are on Team Tisha.

Sharrone, age 35, from Boise says:

My single friends and I have been kicking around the idea of meeting single guys through the Internet. We've heard horror stories and none of us want to be the first in our group to try it! But it seems like there are no eligible single men around anymore. Are we playing with fire?

MYTH #10: *Internet dating is dangerous and irresponsible, and only the really desperate single people find dates there.*

First of all, Sharrone, I know you're not kidding about finding eligible bachelors in Boise. Boise has one of the smallest concentrations of single men in the United States.[5] So unless you travel a lot, your odds at finding a mate are better if you use a resource like the Internet. Of course you could always move to the Los Angeles area where there are reportedly 40,000 more single men than women![6]

But let's address this myth that Internet dating is dangerous, irresponsible, and just plain desperate behavior. Truthfully, you're more likely to slip and fall in your bathroom before you find yourself in physical peril with someone you meet on the Internet. Meeting your soul mate the old-fashioned way sounds very romantic, and it may be the most desirable way to meet your future husband, but sometimes it's just not possible. Taking this extra step to advance a relationship doesn't make you irresponsible (or desperate). It makes you proactive! There are thousands of married, engaged, and happily dating people who met on Web sites such as eHarmony and Match.com.

They probably wouldn't care if someone called them desperate for trying Internet dating because it worked for them, and they are with the one they love!

Many of us have lives crammed with activities, but opportunities to meet other single people just aren't there for a variety of reasons. So be willing to take some chances, Sharrone. That's what life is all about. You can meet a lot of wonderful and interesting people, and you're guaranteed to have lots of great stories to tell as well.

What's Next?

As we move into the next important chapter, let's have a quick discussion about the differences between men and women—don't tell me you hadn't noticed! It all boils down to accepting the fact that we have different ways of communicating and learning how the other half does it. You can thank me later!

CHAPTER TWO

Born to Be Different

Grab a thesaurus and look up all the entries for the word *different*. You'll find words like *dissimilar, separate, abnormal, inconsistent, uncommon, clashing, opposed,* and even *weird*. They all have such negative connotations! But why do we think different is such a bad thing?

The poet and activist Audre Lorde said, "Sometimes we could not bear the face of each other's differences because of what we feared it might say about ourselves."

How do we live in this churning amalgamation of a world with vastly merging cultures and a volatile political landscape when we can't appreciate the differences in other people? We must see something in them that we fear or distrust. We don't understand their ways, so we shrink from them. If we are to have any hope at all of living in harmony, we have to come to an understanding about how others' differences can affect and enhance our own lives.

Let's look at the world of business. Some people are great goal setters and can cast a vision for many to pursue. Others are better at problem solving and supporting a common goal as a team member. Some problem solvers are very aggressive and attack a problem head-on with trial and error, while others take a more passive, analytical approach. On a personal level, some people are socially energetic and can form new relationships almost spontaneously, while others take a lot of time to get to know someone new.

Studies show that we are, in fact, *born* with many of these human attributes. We are born with many natural tendencies that, if understood correctly and embraced, can be our greatest strengths and can also be great blessings to others.

It's when we don't understand natural differences that relationships and teamwork fail to meet their potential—especially when it comes to the differences between men and women in romantic relationships. All men and women are either born with or develop many similar desires and attributes. But there are vital and very often unrecognized natural differences between men and women as well. Being aware of these differences and embracing them will go a long way in developing lasting and growing friendships, partnerships, courtships, and even marriages.

2

Vive la Différence!

Be gentle with one another, sensitive.
Forgive one another as quickly and thoroughly
as God in Christ forgave you.

Ephesians 4:32 msg

∾

Appearing confident is everything to Roland. I see him every Sunday at church and every other Friday morning in counseling about his dating life (or the lack thereof!). I can safely say that even when he looks confident approaching a young lady after church, his heart is pounding like a drum and his knees are buckling. Women think he is so bold and confident that they let him initiate every conversation. I've never seen a woman approach him! What women don't know about Roland is that he is definitely scared.

Sometimes I want to stand up and give a sermon on Roland's behalf. If I could have the undivided attention of every single woman in the congregation, this is what I would say: "Look, ladies, when you see Roland over there stepping up to the plate, could you just appear to be a little more of an opportunity to him? He's trying so hard! And if you knew how nerve-wracking it is for him to approach you, you'd give the guy a chance! I know for a fact that some of you are interested in Roland. So why don't you give the guy a break? It's definitely a way you can distinguish yourself from the rest of the crowd."

I tell Roland, "There's nothing wrong with you. Men gravitate toward places where they feel they'll succeed. We back away from places where we believe we'll fail. We don't waste our investment on failure, so when we see signs of potential success, we're there!"

I've been counseling with a few single women who attend church with Roland, and I've been giving them a similar message as the one I've been giving Roland: "Just package yourself as uncomplicated, confident, and available. Do that and he will definitely show up!"

Something magnificent happened in the Garden of Eden. God created something that would linger throughout time as one of the most beautiful, baffling, controversial, sought-after, exciting, and heartbreaking of all things ever created. Yes, God created man and then He created woman, and even though those feats alone are nothing short of miraculous, God created both man and woman from the same basic design. Both have two arms, two legs, the same basic internal organs—the sameness makes them quite compatible in many ways.

But the *differences* God built into men and women really set the game in motion. If Adam and Eve were exactly the same in every way; sharing the same bodies, thoughts, emotions, attitudes, ambitions—then what would that have accomplished? Pursuing love and relationships today wouldn't be nearly as interesting, wouldn't you agree? The fact is—as Adam and Eve very quickly discovered—men and women are different beyond words!

It is a common enough case; that of a man being suddenly captivated by a woman nearly the opposite of his ideal.

GEORGE ELIOT

We'll explore these vital differences throughout this book because I think taking an honest look at what makes a man tick and what makes a woman content are important to your life as one who is dating and trying to recognize your soul mate. As you read the next chapters, understanding your differences will make your journey easier.

To begin, let's spend a little time in the Word and establish a solid understanding of God's initial plan and design for how He created *you*.

God's Big Idea

When God created you, His great intention was to place upon you His *image* and His *likeness*. But what do we know about His image? Let's go to the Bible to find out. Genesis 1:26 says, "Then God said, 'Let us make human beings in our image and likeness' " (NCV).

We see God's intention to make us like Him. But we also see that He said "let *us*," and that implies He wasn't alone in the creation process! The "us" God mentions consists of the three persons of the Trinity: the Father, the Son, and the Holy Spirit. An intimate relationship existed between the persons of the Trinity, and God is represented to us in those three persons. I won't dwell too heavily on explaining the Trinity, but this is important for you to understand in relation to how the connection of the three is similar to the connections we build with other people. So I recommend that you read books that explain the Holy Trinity and the relationships between the three persons.[7]

My point is, despite some of the necessary similarities that should be present in a relationship, God's intention is that you don't have to be exactly like your mate. Created in His image means you can have deep intimacy with someone who is different from you. But then God went one step further. Look at Genesis 2:7: "Then the LORD God formed the man from the dust of the ground. He breathed the breath of life into the man's nostrils, and the man became a living person" (NLT).

God was in a perfect state of mind when He made you, when He shaped you as male or female. In spite of all your differences, He turned you loose on the planet to have desires and the ability to have intimate relationships with each other.

You are about to venture into an exciting new way to think about your season of singleness. We'll discover more about how men and women often talk at cross-purposes in chapter four. And understanding and accepting your differences will help you immeasurably in the Approach and Be Approachable stage explained in chapter seven. But keeping this information in mind as you read through the book will help you understand the opposite sex more clearly, making you a better partner and communicator.

What's Next?

Next, we'll take a moment to consider the difference between wants and needs, and then get down to the work of defining what's important to you in terms of finding a compatible companion.

CHAPTER THREE

Want Versus Need

Before you can take the first step toward your special "one," let's address a common misconception—the difference between what you *want* and what you *need*.

Love isn't about meeting a need. All your needs are fulfilled in your relationship with the living God. So if God is supplying all your *needs,* then everything else must be a *want.* You need food. You need air. You need water. You need salvation. But you want a companion. You want a relationship. You want someone on this planet to know you and love you in spite of what they know about you.

How many times have you heard someone say, "I *need* you, baby! I can't live without you"? Now you know that's not true. I don't know anyone who ever spontaneously dropped dead because a person to whom they had a strong emotional attachment left the relationship.

When you feel like you can't live without someone and you let them know that, you've created a no-win situation for them and for yourself. You've asked them to become your food, water, and air.

You can't do that with another person. If you pour your entire life into a man, pin all your hopes and dreams on his ability to make you happy, and expect him to perform flawlessly according to your image of him, your dreams will be shattered. Bishop T.D. Jakes says, "An unhappy single woman will be an unhappy married woman."

And, men, if you hold on to your woman like she's your high school basketball trophy, you convince her that she has to be perfect for you, and you can't stand on your own two feet without her, then you've created a weak seam in the fabric of her feminine strength.

Our world needs strong women in relationships. We also need men who can be themselves without unrealistic expectations and demands placed upon them.

So, here's the big difference between want and need: If I recognize that I don't need you, then I'm free to love you in a responsible way. When you have the want-versus-need issue out of the way, you can relax. You don't have to say, "I need someone I can understand!" You can say, "I want someone I can understand."

Making an idol of another human is a sin. Make Jesus the Lover of your soul and you'll be free to love another human being in a way that will set you both free from any hint of idol worship.

3

Define What You Want

A man's heart plans his way,
But the LORD directs his steps.

PROVERBS 16:9

❧

Cheri sits in my office and wrings a tissue in her small hands. She says she doesn't want to grow old alone, but every time a man asks her out on a date, she freezes. "It's always the same," she says, "I date a guy for about a month, and then I have to end it. I just know it's never going to work." Finally we pray together and ask God to reveal to her the source of her anxiety.

Three days later Cheri stands in my office, a smile beaming radiantly across her face. "I know what it is!" she exclaims. Cheri reveals to me that her heart has been a blank slate—no expectations, no demands. She's been living in a constant state of relationship inertia.

"What does this mean, Cheri?" I ask even though I already know the answer. Her response is music to my ears. "I'm not going to find my soul mate if I haven't decided what he should look like. And I can't know what he looks like if I don't know what I want."

You can't recognize your soul mate unless you've taken the time to define what he or she will look like—on the inside and on the outside. But that's a destination you can't reach until you know *yourself* better. In this chapter, you're going to mentally define and refine yourself and your perfect mate so when that person comes into your life, you won't have to wonder or have anxiety about whether he or she is *the one*. You're going to know because you already took the time to understand your own heart, and you've already carved a picture of that person on it.

First, Know Thyself

There are many things to know about yourself and about what you're looking for in a relationship. For example:

- Are you looking for a spouse or just someone to casually date?

- How long do you think you'd want to date someone before you think you'd be ready to commit to marriage?

- Are you mentally and emotionally mature enough to handle a dating relationship?

- What about a long-term relationship?

- Are you mature enough to handle the sex issue when it comes up?

- Are your dating skills up to date?

- How much should you tell another person about yourself on a first, second, and third date?

And this doesn't even begin to address important side issues like finances and family—things that may seem incidental in light of a love relationship but actually can loom very large as time goes on. (If you've ever dated someone your mama disapproved of, you'll know what I mean!) Let's take a moment to really think this thing through.

Strengths, Weaknesses, Opportunities, Threats

In business there is a common marketing model that helps managers determine strengths, weaknesses, opportunities, and possible threats. Let's spend a little time on this model by compiling a list of your strengths and weaknesses. Then we'll make a list of your potential opportunities. The final step of this model is to make a list of potential threats. The bad news is that there will *always* be threats (such as "I could make a huge mistake!" or "I could hook up with a real dog!"), but the good news is that your list of threats is the same as everyone else's. It's all part of the risk of dating. You can't avoid the risks, but you can learn to wisely identify them so you'll know how to manage them when, not if, they occur.

Now, let's hone your list of strengths and weaknesses to razor-sharp clarity and find out where you excel and where you need some work. Remember to define these in terms of finding a relationship.

Defining Your Strengths and Weaknesses

Your Strengths. A good marketer knows all the strengths of his or her product. Just pick up any newspaper and pull out the sales inserts. The advertisements all have one common feature—bullet points drawing the eye to the benefits or strengths of the product. What are your strengths—your bullet points? List five below:

1. _____

2. _____

3. _____

4. _____

5. _____

Now list five positive adjectives that describe you. These adjectives can describe you physically, emotionally, socially, and mentally. Be honest, and remember that this is the *good* stuff about you.

1. _____

2. _____

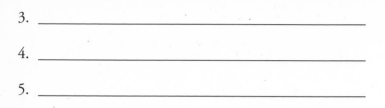

3. _____

4. _____

5. _____

Now write a short, one-paragraph description of yourself as a whole. Try to include all five positive adjectives in your paragraph. Be sure to write in first person ("I am energetic and I love people.") because you speak life into yourself with words. This short statement is your "strengths statement." It's the strongest negotiating instrument you bring to every relationship table.

Your Weaknesses. Pull out the newspaper advertisements again and find the fine print. It reveals the weaknesses: 21 percent interest, no grace period, not valid with other offers, offer expires after a certain date, and so on. Because the weaknesses are in small print and not in the same glaring large print as the strengths we prefer to see, they may be hard to notice at first glance. Nevertheless they are there and you can't ignore them.

So what's *your* fine print? List five negative adjectives that describe you. These are your flaws. Don't worry, everyone has them. Knowing your flaws will help you compensate for or eliminate them.

1. _____

2. _____

3. _____

4. _____

5. _____

Now write a short, one-paragraph description of your weaknesses as a whole. Try to include all five negative adjectives. In this exercise, do *not* write in first person. Write about your weaknesses and flaws as if they are detached from you ("Jealousy and possessiveness are dangerous."). Just call them what they are, but don't call yourself names with them. This short statement is your "weaknesses statement"—your small print. It's the strongest negotiating instrument Satan will bring to the relationship table to keep you from achieving your goals.

Maximizing Your Strengths and Minimizing Your Weaknesses. Let's look at a process for creating some strong "power improvement" statements about you.

Review your lists of five strengths and five weaknesses, then put them together in power improvement statements. For instance, if you wrote down "honest" as a core strength and "controlling" as a core weakness, you might write, "Controlling others is manipulative, but I am an honest person so I can see I have this problem. I confess it right now and vow to make every effort to stop myself when I'm too overbearing. I am going to let go of my need to control every situation."

Try to cover every strength and every weakness, and feel free to combine as many as you like. I think you'll find that you have strengths that can minimize or even help eliminate many of your weaknesses. Here's another example. If you wrote down "compassionate" as a core strength and "obsessive-compulsive" as a core weakness, you might write, "I have a tendency to exhibit obsessive-compulsive behavior in some circumstances, and that's not healthy. But I'm also very compassionate. I'm going to extend a little of the grace I give to others to myself so that I don't have to obsess about things like housekeeping or neatness or other people's idiosyncrasies."

Complete this exercise in the space provided and then continue on to the next section.

Defining Your Opportunities and Threats

Your Opportunities. You can leverage your strengths to create opportunities, pursue leads, and move you toward your goals. If your strengths are values like honesty and stability, there are opportunities abounding for you in relationships. After all, everyone wants someone who is honest and stable. You define your opportunities so you can see where your strengths will lead you.

Now I want you to list five prospective opportunities you have to meet people and show them the strengths you detailed previously. This list might include common-interest clubs or meetings, local supermarkets or malls, school, work—anywhere you might find potential partners. You probably have a very busy social life, but narrow this list down to the best places or events you can maximize your exposure and demonstrate your top five strengths. Look for any hidden opportunities you may have overlooked in the past.

For example, if you've identified a sense of humor as one of your strengths, the grocery store may not be the best place to show it off! But that sense of humor might come in handy if you volunteer as a docent at the local museum or try out for a part with your local community theater.

Complete this exercise in the space provided and then continue on to the next section.

1. _____

2. _____

3. _____

4. _____

5. _____

Your Threats. One caution: You can inadvertently leverage your weaknesses to invite threats into your pursuits. If, for instance, you are a woman who leans toward rescuing broken-down losers, you risk the threat of ending up in a bad relationship where you're more of a caretaker than a partner. Men, if one of your weaknesses is being too controlling, then a threat to your pursuits could be a long string of short-term flings that leave you feeling empty and alone. I want you to learn to recognize your threats so you can see where your weaknesses will lead *you* if you don't lead *them*.

List five potential threats to your relationship efforts. I'm looking for very specific threats that relate to your top five weaknesses. For instance, if you have a weakness for gambling, then a threat might be dating someone who works in a casino.

Complete this exercise in the space provided and then continue on to the next section.

1. _____

2. _____

3. _____

4. _____

5. _____

Maximizing Your Opportunities and Minimizing Your Threats. Understanding the relationship between cause and effect will help you succeed in many areas of your life—especially relationships. Developing these skills takes time and patience. Because you shouldn't be in a big hurry to get married, you have the opportunity to take time to work on polishing your strengths.

But the most important lesson in this exercise is gaining an understanding of the cause and effect of your weaknesses because they create situations and environments that can doom you to repeated failure, a never-ending cycle of unhappiness, codependency, and even abuse. Those who don't learn from history are doomed to repeat it! I don't want that for you. You can use these exercises to stop your weakness cycles and become an informed and intelligent person whose relationship dreams come true.

Know What You Want

The introspective lesson in the first part of this chapter helped determine if you're ready for the big leap into a love relationship. If you feel you've faced your weaknesses and you're ready for the opportunities and even the threats that await you, then let's move on to defining what you want in a partner.

Another common business tool is what's known as *segmentation*. Segmentation will help you determine two very different things— what you can live with in a partner (things that are negotiable) and what you can't live without (these are definite deal-breakers in the relationship).

Defining What You Can Live With

List ten things you would like your potential partner to have. They can be physical or emotional traits, social behaviors, or mental attitudes. Be honest and don't worry about sounding too presumptuous or demanding. You may even want to start with more than ten things and narrow them down to your top ten. Be sure these ten things are all *negotiable*. For example you might say, "I'd like him to be over six feet tall." However, you're not planning to limit yourself to men who stand over the six-foot mark. It's just something you'd prefer.

As you make your list, keep in mind your strengths and weaknesses. Meditate on the qualities, characteristics, beliefs, core values, and physical aspects of the person you believe would be a good match for your strengths and weaknesses.

Take a breather and walk away from your list for a while. Pray about it. Talk to some close friends about it. Then come back and see if your list needs revising.

Complete this exercise in the space provided and then continue on to the next section.

1. _____

2. _____

3. _____

4. _____

5. _____

6. _____

7. _____

8. _____

9. _____

10. _____

Defining What You Can't Live Without

List ten things that absolutely, positively must be present in a partner for you to consider a long-term relationship with him or her. (Or, conversely, you can list things that a partner absolutely cannot have in order for you to be interested in them. For example, you might say your partner cannot, under any circumstances, drink alcohol.) Remember, this list can contain physical or emotional traits, social behaviors, or mental attitudes. You might say, "The woman I am looking for must want to have my children." If you're absolutely certain that it's non-negotiable, then write it down.

As you make your list, again keep in mind your strengths and weaknesses. Meditate on the qualities, characteristics, beliefs, core values, and physical aspects of the person you believe would be a good match for you. If you have a tendency to fall for addictive personalities, then put this on your nonnegotiable list of things to avoid, and don't budge on it! Keep your eye on healthy, productive relationships and stay off the *Jerry Springer Show!*

I seriously recommend that you pray over this list and talk to your closest friends about it. Remember, this list details the nonnegotiable things you want in a partner.

Complete this exercise in the space provided and then continue on to the next section.

1. _____

2. _____

3. _____

4. _____

5. _____

6. _____

7. _____

8. _____

9. _____

10. _____

Dr. Ronn

Defining What You Want

I counsel a lot of single people who are wracked with confusion about dating and marriage. I do my best to assure them that there is nothing wrong with just wanting to date. And there's nothing wrong with wanting to get married. In fact, if it's their choice, there's nothing wrong with not wanting to date *or* get married.

One of the biggest obstacles you face as a single person is that if you don't know what you want, people will keep approaching you with what *they* want. You'll get caught up in their desires and before you know it, another month goes by, and then another year. Don't waste another five minutes on a relationship that God didn't intend for you to have.

Determining Feasibility

After you've created your lists of ten negotiable and ten nonnegotiable traits, sit down with your Bible and spend some time with the Lord. Ask Him if you are being reasonable and prudent. For instance, if you listed long hair as a nonnegotiable trait, then think about this: Did God say your mate should have long or short hair? Nowhere in the Bible will you find God telling you that. But God did say something about whether or not your mate should be saved. Be wise, He says, and pick fruit from the correct tree.

Pray over your lists before you commit them to substance. Be prepared to change your mind and move some of your nonnegotiables into the negotiable list. You have to leave certain options open. The goal of this exercise is to draw closer to God, His purpose for you, and the partner He's chosen for you.

Once you've completed your lists, post them in a visible place—on your refrigerator, bathroom mirror, the back of your office door, in your car or briefcase. Whenever you feel uncertain about your choices, or if you feel yourself floating off course a little (or careening dangerously out of control), go to these lists, research Scriptures that support your choices, and get back on track.

What's Next?

You may want to take a short break and prepare for an exciting and introspective adventure into the world of package design. That's right! You're going to learn how you can put your best foot forward by building your best promotional package—you!

CHAPTER FOUR

Lost and Found

"Delight yourself in the LORD and he will give you the desires of your heart. Commit your way to the LORD; trust in him and he will do this." Psalm 37:4-5 NIV

Does this verse mean we should delight ourselves in the Lord and He will give us everything we desire? That sounds like good news, doesn't it? To some this passage may sound as if it's all about them and what they want.

But take another look. God is really saying that *as* you delight in Him, He will place desires *in* you. You'll wonder where these desires came from, and you'll wonder if they are really desires at all! Believe it or not, God knows what is best for you, and that goes for your heart's desires. So learning how to open up that dialogue with God and listen to what He's trying to tell you can mean all the difference in the world between an opportunity lost and a goldmine found.

Sometimes opportunities will pass you by because you weren't paying attention—other times they pass because you were unwilling to do the work to define what you were looking for in that opportunity. You didn't know what it was when you came in contact with it. The opportunity was there all along, a desire God put in you as a result of your delighting in Him.

How many times have you missed the chance to delight in His gifts for you? It's an incredible feeling to know you have a Father who cares that much about your delights. In fact, you should tell Him about it.

4

The Product Is You!

But earnestly desire the greater gifts.
And I show you a still more excellent way.

1 CORINTHIANS 12:31 NASB

∽

James says he doesn't understand why he's had six girlfriends in the past year. "I'm a really good-looking guy, I think. I have a big-time career, and my own home. I know how to treat a woman. Hey, I bought the last chick I dated a Rolex for her birthday or something. She got upset over some stupid girl I was talking to at her party. Whatever."

While James is talking, I'm making notes: "the last chick he dated...Rolex...her birthday or something...some stupid girl...whatever." The problems are obvious—to me.

James doesn't have a clue that his packaging is deceiving. What he needs is a crash course in how to repackage himself, and that's going to mean a lot of education. I know I can help him. I just wonder if he's ready. I say to him, "James, the way you develop new habits is by putting them into action. And as you consistently put them into action, it's funny how quickly your emotions catch up with reality."

Ask yourself these questions: Is your package perfect the way it is? Or is there something (or several things) about your package you need to change? My experience tells me no one is perfect and everyone has something to learn about love.

James's problem was that he packaged himself as "all that" and he didn't bother to try and understand anything about what a woman wants. So clearly James wasn't "all that." In fact, he wasn't even half that. But two years later, James is engaged to a wonderful and fantastic woman named Cassandra. Today, he's pretty close to "all that." What James successfully learned about how to repackage himself is what you're going to learn right now.

What the World Sees

You get to decide how the world sees you. The clothes you wear, the things you do, even whether or not you laugh at a joke—all can be seen by others who will then form a perception of who you are based on what they've observed. Your true behaviors, beliefs, and core values can't be hidden from a potential mate for long. You can have all the style and personality of a Hollywood star, but when you finally get close to someone, what you believe and what you value will eventually show through the superficial spit and polish. These deeper, less often seen factors will determine how you really view the opposite sex, how you treat them, and ultimately, how they respond to you.

On a grander scale, Paul told the Corinthians that their gifts were great, but exercising their gifts in love was greater, and he set out to teach them a better way (1 Corinthians 12:31). You, too, can learn a better way—a way to exercise your gifts in love so that what you give to the world is the very best you.

Learning the Better Way

The verse quoted at the beginning of this chapter, 1 Corinthians 12:31, introduces us to the "love chapter" of the Bible (chapter 13). It's a chapter I highly recommend you read if you're thinking about falling in love! But John 3:16 tells us what real love is. It's not how we loved God, but how He loved us and gave us something precious. He loved us so much He gave His only begotten Son.

True love is when you give someone the kind of love they need, even if it's not the kind of love *you* need. The kind of love God has shown to us is the kind of love He wants us to give to each other.

This is generally a harder lesson for men to grasp because we won't usually come right out and tell women specifically what love feels like. We operate in the world of actions and goals—but that doesn't mean a woman with her feminine ways can't capture our hearts and become the object of our undivided attention. Women, on the other hand, don't usually have a problem communicating with us. Men, you'll definitely get the message—even if it seems like some kind of cryptic message you'll have to have cracked by a retired World War II Navajo code talker.

The better way doesn't have to be complicated. If you're motivated rightly, you can discover the secrets locked in the hearts of men and women who long to be known by their soul mates.

The truth is that we all look for certain things when we are searching for a lifetime mate. If we find these things—and find them in abundance—we'll pursue that special person to the ends of the earth. If we spend a little time with someone and find him or her lacking in the important areas, we'll move on. In order to get and hold your heart's desire, you need to add some important elements to your package (your life) that will make you a greater asset to the relationship.

Add These Items to Your Package

Learning Love and Respect. Dr. Emerson Eggerichs wrote an amazing book a few years ago called _Love and Respect_.[8] In his book Dr. Eggerichs echoes a premise as old as human life on earth—one that I've taught often and even wrote about in my book _An Outrageous Commitment_.

Basically the premise is that men and women have two different sets of needs. Both needs are met only when a woman gives her man the kind of love _he_ requires, and likewise, as he is fulfilled, he gives his woman the kind of love _she_ requires—sometimes even unconsciously. The wonderful part is that it doesn't matter who starts this process, but when it happens, inevitably both partners get the kind of love that speaks directly to them.

For men, the respect issue is very simple. Yet for a lot of women, it may be very difficult to grasp. A man needs to be respected. The word respect comes from the Latin word *respicere,* which means "look at, regard, consider." And *respicere,* broken down into two parts, looks like this:

re—again, anew

specere—look, see

Given the type of man God made—the task- and goal-oriented tender and keeper—He put inside a man the need to be looked at, regarded, and considered again and again. Thus we understand why a man likes to be applauded and commended for his work at tending and keeping. We also understand why he feels the need to be continuously regarded for his opinions.

So *respect* him, ladies. Don't do it just because it makes him feel good or because you'll ultimately get something out of it. Do it because God commands it. He really does! Go to Ephesians 5:33. It says, "A wife must respect her husband" (NCV).

Treat a man as if he were what he ought to be and you help him become what he is capable of being.

JOHANN WOLFGANG VON GOETHE

Many women, especially those who have had bad experiences with men, will say, "Well, he doesn't *deserve* my respect. He has to *earn* it." Not true! He may have to earn your trust, he may have to earn a place in your heart, and he may have to earn the honor of marrying you, but respect should not be something he has to earn from you. I know I risk angering a lot of women by delivering this message, but before you can expect to find a man who will love you with the same kind of God-mandated love you crave, you must get this teaching about respect into your spirit. It's one of the hardest parts of preparing for a love relationship, but once you accept it, you won't have to revisit it in times of trouble.

The flip side of the Ephesians command is that men are mandated to love their wives. Every woman wants a man who truly loves women. I suppose this can be taken several ways. Yes, women want a man who is a heterosexual and looking for a long-term love relationship with a woman. No, a woman doesn't want a man who loves *all* women—at least to the point where he wants to love them all at once! What I'm getting at is that a woman needs to know that the man in her life has a deep and abiding affection, love, and respect for the women in his life.

A man who makes demeaning remarks about his mother or sister—or other women in general—will not make a good husband. Having children, especially daughters, with a man like that would be very irresponsible. A man who uses vulgarity to describe women or makes degrading jokes about them would not be a good date to bring home to the family.

There are a lot of dogs out there who honestly think it's okay to bash women in front of others. If you're one of those men and you're saying, "Hey, my girl laughs when I do it. I don't see a problem here," I'll be honest with you. It's not funny, it's not appropriate, and it's definitely not love-talk to a woman. You need to check your vocabulary and your intentions at the door and make sure your attitude regarding women is in the right place. If there is a part of you that has been so damaged by a woman in your life that you have to resort to disrespecting women in that manner, then get thee to a counselor! You don't have to relate that way anymore. That attitude is holding you back from a lasting relationship.

A woman wants a man who is attentive to his mother's needs, feelings, and wishes—a man who cherishes his mother. She wants a man who is protective and loving with his sisters (without being pushy, nosey, or controlling). She wants a man who respects his female business associates. Most of all, she wants a man who will always be loyal and speak of her with respect, no matter where he is or whom he's with. A man like this is prized among women because they know he will be a good partner, an excellent husband, and a loving dad.

If you're in a dating relationship now, and even if there's no talk of marriage yet, you must learn, understand, and practice the Ephesians mandate of love and respect. If you do this now, you will enjoy the fruit of a great harvest.

Tony's Story
THE TRUTH ABOUT PORNOGRAPHY

Pornography comes in many forms and can be found as easily as turning on your computer and, in a lot of cases, the television. Tony sees me twice a week to talk about his addiction to pornography and how it affects his relationship with his girlfriend, Janet. He talks about his childhood, finding the "innocent" *Playboy* in his dad's bathroom and giggling over it. He talks about the "old days" of casual sex and glib attempts at promises made during one-night-stands.

My counsel is difficult for him to hear. I tell him, "Tony, if you're a man taken captive by Christ, then you're *not* a man taken captive by pornography. If you're sneaking around behind Janet's back, looking at porn on the Internet, having cybersex with other women (if they really *are* women), and skulking in the backdoor of adult bookstores, then you're being unfaithful to Janet and to God. You're acting like an orphan, a slave to sin, and if you don't stop, it will destroy you."

Months of prayer and counseling bring progress, but then he has an inevitable setback. It's like starting all over again. My heart breaks for him, for Janet, and their future, if he doesn't stop.

This is one of the worst possible ways Tony can damage his relationship with Janet because it's an insidious disease that won't just go away over time. Tony won't just grow out of it. It's a cancer that will grow until it can't be contained. It's a drug he has become addicted to, and after a while he'll need something with a little more kick than the last experience to keep him going. His father didn't realize that the "innocent" pornography is now leading his son to harder forms of pornography and other types of addictions. Tony also has a problem with drinking. Other men I counsel about pornography often times have extended addictions to gambling, drinking, drug use...even domestic abuse.

It's two steps forward and one step back for Tony. But we make progress every week. We pray. We fight it together. I have great faith that he'll conquer this demon once and for all.

Learning the Proper Doses of Criticism and Applause. You can give out the kind of love that fits your mate, and package yourself as someone who is very good at it only by making sure every criticism you might have is followed by a commendation.

Complaining and criticizing are part of every relationship, but if you can temper that with an equal amount of applause for other things, you'll be showing love in a way that will always surprise your partner. The goal is to reach a place where the applause is multiplied, outweighing the complaining and criticizing.

Some folks can't help themselves though. They say, "My mama told me to always say what's on my mind. And I have to let him have it over this because my blood pressure is going up!" That's fine—to a degree. But remember this: If you are packaging yourself in a way that does not represent what is truly in you, then you are working against your own relationship success!

Complaints and criticism are not the only things inside of you. So here's a simple rule that will help you break bad news: Lead with the applause, and if you must, then follow with the criticism. But speak that truth in love. The behavior you reward will be the behavior repeated.

The power of a man's virtue should not be measured by his special efforts, but by his ordinary doing.

BLAISE PASCAL

Learning How to Share the Adventure. We all have an inherent need to look out for number one and, to a degree, think about yourself. In fact, you *should* take care of yourself. You can't help someone who is stalled on the side of the road if you're already there with an empty tank, right?

Roberto says:

My girlfriend wakes up and goes to sleep listening to WIFM (What's In It For Me). Sure, she accepts my gifts and lets me spend a lot of money on her, but she won't take any of my advice or suggestions, and she never asks me what I want or need. If things don't change, our relationship is over.

When you're in true relationship with another person, you have to be able to accept assistance, gifts, suggestions and advice, instruction, and love with grace. Remember that a man is utilitarian in nature, and he wants to feel useful to a woman. Accepting his help and even his burdens with grace makes a woman very attractive to him.

Likewise, you have to be able to *give* those things to your partner with an even larger dose of grace. The greatest enemy to love is selfishness, and you never know when it's going to appear and wreck your efforts to build a successful relationship.

Selfishness is something you can't hide for very long. Fixing your eyes so firmly on yourself that you can't see what your partner needs will ultimately result in one thing: The person you think of the most will be the person you wind up with—you!

The ultimate goal of a relationship is moving from a self-centered life to an other-centered life. Another beautiful aspect of being other-centered is being able to invite another person into your personal adventure.

Men measure real strength by how much they can accomplish on their own. Women measure strength by how much they can get done together. A woman naturally wants to be helpful to the man in her life. The Bible, after all, said God gave man a "help" mate when He created woman.

In many cases a woman will need a man's help with something before a man needs to ask for a woman's help, but it's a woman's desire to know she's indispensable and irreplaceable to her man.

In his book *Wild at Heart,* author John Eldredge talks about a man inviting his woman "into his adventure."[9] He says every man wants an adventure to live and every woman wants to be invited into that adventure with him. I realize there are many women who certainly don't need a man to have an adventure, but Eldredge's premise is true on many levels.

For a woman, being invited into her man's adventure is far more than just packing a man's briefcase and having it waiting by the door when he goes to work. It's more than balancing his checkbook or organizing his closet. It's rather condescending to think she lives for those sorts of activities. She may do those things, and many more things, "just because," but they can hardly be considered adventures. A woman wants to be a part of the big things in her man's life, the things that mean a great deal to him.

Lauren's Story
FEELING LEFT OUT

"I feel so empty in my relationship with Derrick. He doesn't understand how much it hurts me to be left out of his life, especially when he's having so much strife in his new law practice."

Lauren has been dating Derrick for almost a year. They live in different cities and only see each other on weekends, so I know how valuable she considers their time together. "I understand," I tell Lauren. "You long to help him in a way that makes his life indescribably easier."

"Yes," she says, "but he doesn't depend on me for anything. I would love it if just once he would ask for my help. It's not that I want to take full responsibility away from him, but it would make me feel like I've been invited into part of his world."

"You want him to confide in you and trust you with some of his confidences?"

"That would be nice, but he doesn't share anything with me."

I explained to her that Derrick is obviously one of those men who has a hard time opening up. "Perhaps the longer he knows you, the easier it will be for him to identify your strengths and see where you fit into his life."

"We've been dating for almost a year. How long does it take?"

"That, Lauren, is for you to decide."

John Eldredge also says every woman is a beauty to be rescued. A lot of women don't feel they need to be rescued, as if they can't get by on their own or they can't live without a man sweeping in and saving them each and every day. But I don't think Eldredge meant it so literally. "Rescue" can mean a lot of things to a woman. One of the definitions of the word is to be "called out." She is a beautiful creature of God that wants a special light shined upon her—one that calls her out and invites her to something greater. She wants to step forward and take her place in the great adventure of life, including the great unknowns of life.

If a man can package himself as that light and call the woman he loves out into more and greater life purposes, then he is one special man indeed. Any woman would be thrilled to be invited into his life.

Blaze's Story
Ms. Independent

Blaze is a woman with the rare gift of being very male-friendly. She has many male friends who gravitate toward her—not necessarily sexually or romantically—but because they feel comfortable around her. Blaze was raised with five brothers and several other male family members. "I'm just comfortable around men," she says.

Blaze counsels with me because, she says, "I can't find a man who is secure enough to handle my independence." I tell Blaze that men find it easy to befriend her, telling her things they wouldn't normally tell other women. Why men can relate so easily to her is probably very baffling to them. I tell her she's special that way. "But," I say, "your greatest gift is also an obstacle for you because you can inadvertently come across as if there is nothing a man can bring to your life."

I know this about men: They want to know that if they show up with their tools, they will be asked to use them. They want to know that there is something valuable and unique they can bring to the table. And I know this about Blaze: She doesn't need a man's money—in fact there may not be much of anything she needs from a man because she's so self-sufficient. I want to help her understand that if her man knows he can show up with something she *does* need—something she can give him credit for providing— then she's just made him the happiest man in the world.

Then Blaze loses it. "What is this thing about men? I have

my own house. I have my own car. I have a good job. And I make twice as much money as most men. I think men are just intimidated by me. They just can't handle it because they are insecure."

"Yes," I tell her, "there are some men like that. But that's not usually the case. And that's not usually the problem. It's not that men can't handle it or that they're intimidated by your success. When you package yourself as someone who doesn't need *anything* from a man and imply that there is *nothing* you can give him credit for having brought into the relationship, then you've taken the action away from him. If he can't find a way to make a measurable difference in your life and get some applause for doing it, then he'll likely pack up his tools and go looking for another task to handle."

It was like watching a lightbulb come on in Blaze's eyes.

Learning the Two Universal Languages. For a man who plans his actions and likes to follow through to the next thing, being with a woman who will help him move from point A to point B is a blessing to him. His perfect woman understands that now that he has said the words "I love you," he's ready for something bigger, splashier, more fun, more serious, and more substantial than the last thing they did together. It's all linear movement for men, and they approach relationships just like they do everything else in life—like it's an important job to do.

===== *Linda says:* =====

I know he can share his feelings because when we were first dating, we had these conversations where he or I would call and say "I just called to say hi and now I've got to go to work." The next thing you know we are on the phone for six hours! So I know he can share.

When a relationship begins, a man typically *tells* his woman how he feels. After that's been successfully completed, he starts looking for ways to *show* her how he feels. *Saying* is the first stage of the relationship—*showing* comes next. That's why a relationship for him begins with writing poetry, sending e-mails with the scripture of the day, and leaving messages such as, "I've never experienced anything like this! It's so amazing that the Lord has put you on this planet for me to find you! Now I'm looking forward to all the ways in which God will knit our hearts and minds and ways and wills together!" But after God has done the knitting of the hearts and minds and ways and wills, there may not be a whole lot of poetry and e-mails. That's not because he doesn't love her anymore. It's just the linear progression to the *next* thing for him.

And if a man can appreciate a woman who is able to understand that, then he should be more than willing to sign up for an advanced class in how to read between her lines.

===== *Michael says:* =====

We had a conversation yesterday…I *think* it was a conversation. Honestly, I can't even tell you what it was about. I just know she was upset about something I didn't do. The whole time she was talking, I was thinking to myself, *Does she even know why she's upset?* I couldn't figure it out. Pretty soon, I just had to tune her out. And I felt bad about that because I wanted to understand what she was really saying. It was so frustrating! It was as if we were not even speaking the same language.

Yes, men, it's hard to know where the lines are, but I'm going to share a very simple technique with you men that will put you on the fast track to speaking womanese:

1. Listen carefully to everything she says to you. Get out of your own head for a while and pay attention to what she's actually saying.

2. Go to work as a detective and read between the lines of what she says. You'll have to gauge her mood and put what she says into the context of what happened just before the conversation began. Ask her questions and don't get frustrated! If you don't understand something, reassure her of your love and tell her you don't understand.

3. To be sure you understand her, repeat what she said and what you *think* she said by what she *wasn't* saying.

You're probably thinking, *What?! What are you talking about? What she said and what she wasn't saying in what she said or didn't say? Did she say it or not? What language is she speaking?*

I know it's confusing. Women are confusing! But the longer you're together, the more comfortable she'll become sharing things with you in *your* language. It will become easier for you to understand what she's saying—even when she's *not* saying it.

It's hard for men to admit when we don't know something, but we really do need to learn to admit when we don't understand what the women in our lives are saying. A woman would rather share her life with a man who admits that he's clueless than a man who pretends to have all the answers. She doesn't expect you to be able to fill in all the blanks, and she doesn't want you to tell her what she meant to say.

Craig and Lisa's Story
IT'S THE LITTLE THINGS

Craig and Lisa sit in my office. She's angry and he has a worried look on his face. "The other day I told Craig how much I loved him and enjoyed spending time with him. Do you know what he said?" Lisa is fuming. "He said, 'Oh, that's cool. Hey, can you pick up my dry cleaning?'"

This isn't going to be easy. Craig and Lisa have been dating for two years and have just started premarital counseling. The wedding date is five months away. During my last session alone with Craig, he told me he didn't get the promotion he was hoping for at work. It struck him hard, even though he's usually a very positive and self-assured man. Lisa knew about the promotion, and was very supportive, but Craig still felt down about it.

I ask Lisa, "Have you noticed that Craig responds to your heartfelt emotions by saying things like, 'How do you like the way I did this or that?' or 'Wasn't that a great restaurant I took you to last weekend?'" Lisa responds, "Yes! He's been doing that a lot lately!" Craig pipes in, "Yeah, you're right. I do that. Is that bad?"

"No, it's not bad, Craig." I tell them both, "Men are wired

for performance. Men naturally savor being recognized, approved, applauded, and admired for all the things they do and how well they do them." I don't mention the promotion because I can tell they are both thinking about it.

The following week, I meet Lisa without Craig. She says, "I tried something different last weekend. It was just a little thing, but the results were huge. Craig picked me up ten minutes early for our date and I told him how much I loved how punctual he was and how much I felt loved by his courtesy toward me." Lisa continued, "He didn't really react with facial expressions or words, but during the evening I could tell he was glowing from the inside out."

"Lisa," I say, "there was actually a parade breaking out inside his chest."

The value of Lisa's total package skyrocketed when she learned that Craig receives love when she expresses her appreciation for what he does. Love, to him, isn't a yellow rose or a Hallmark card. His love for Lisa blossoms when she tells him how great his tie matches his suit, as trivial as that sounds.

Learning to Fight Fair. Most arguments between men and women start and progress because one or both people say something they don't mean, or they make promises they don't intend to keep.

Getting back to the differences in languages, men understand the subtle use of suggestion and symbolism just fine, but they are more literal-minded than women. Sometimes it's hard for a man to wade through a conversation. He might think, *Okay, now what did she mean by that? Did she just say she wants to go to my parents' house instead of her sister's for Thanksgiving? Or is she just giving in for the sake of avoiding an argument? And are we going to have a fight about this later?* Conversely, as rare as it is for a man to say what's deep in his heart, most women might think, *Does he not like my sister? What did she ever do to him? Why do we always have this argument?*

Giving mixed signals about what you want and expect will get you a mixed response, and the cycle of miscommunication will grow and mutate until neither of you understands what the other is saying or meaning.

Allen and Joanna's Story
COMMUNICATING THE REAL ISSUES

Joanna is upset about how much time she and Allen spend apart. He travels a lot with his job, and she spends long hours at her office. She's been moody, emotional, and unable to make Allen understand how she feels.

They started seeing me a couple weeks ago when they first considered breaking off their relationship for a few weeks. They've only been dating six months, and they're both of the opinion that they don't have a lot invested in the relationship, so it wouldn't be a great loss. However, when I meet with them separately, they express such sweet and enduring love for each other. It's clear to me that their relationship can and should be saved. But there's still tension.

"You're always hanging with your buddies or working," Joanna complains. "You *never* spend time with me."

"Why don't you like my friends?" Allen asks defensively. "What's wrong with my friends? And why do you want me to quit my job!"

Throwing a flag into the ring, I offer this suggestion, "I don't think there's anything wrong with your friends, Allen. She doesn't dislike your friends or your job. Do you, Joanna?"

"No, that's not it at all," Joanna says. "It's just that you're *always* with them and *never* with me." We end our session a little more tense than I would like, but Joanna agrees to stay a few minutes longer for a one-on-one session.

"Joanna," I begin, "I know the issue is not his friends or his work. It's that he isn't spending enough time with you. And that's the bottom line, isn't it? You're feeling neglected?"

"Exactly!" Joanna cries. "Why can't Allen see that?"

"You may not want to hear this, Joanna, but Allen can't see it because you're clouding the issue with other things. You're telling him he spends too much time a) at work and b) with his friends. He's going to automatically take your words at face value and think you don't like his friends or his job. But the real issue is that he's not showing you enough attention. You need to look him in the eye and tell him that. Don't throw a bunch of other things into the mix. They will only confuse him about what's really wrong with the relationship. Give him the bottom line. And don't feel bad about wanting more of his time."

"I understand," she says.

"But there is something else, Joanna," I add, "and that is the use of words like *never* and *always*. When you use words like that with a man, you've cornered him into believing his performance is going to be limited to pass or fail, and there will be no chance for him to succeed at pleasing you. He either 'gets it right' with you or he doesn't and he's failed. I know how much you love him. But his fear of failure may be greater than your love at this early stage of your relationship."

I see Allen and Joanna the following week, and even though they're still not sure they'll be together six months from now, they agree they're going to try to work it out. I can't say they'll make it, but when I see two people who love each other this much and are working this hard at it, I feel very confident that God will show up for them.

Another source of contention stems from simply not having the courage of your convictions. If you make a promise to someone—whether it's to your partner, a family member, or a coworker—keep that promise. When you say you're going to do something, do it.

In the beginning of a dating relationship, men are serious can-do creatures. They make promises and they deliver with flying colors. But as time passes, his colors may fade to a more passive pastel. Gone are the dramatic flairs that were meant to impress her and win her heart. Yes, men are task-oriented and once we've accomplished something, we like to move on to the next thing. We want women to understand that about us.

But the rule here is very simple for both men and women: We should not deliver the goods on things we don't plan to continue delivering. Consistency is more important than the deed itself. Men, if you do those special things because she's worth it, then you must continue doing them as long as you feel she's worth it. If you come to a place in the dating relationship where you don't feel she's worth it anymore, it's unfair to stick around and fake it. End the relationship.

Sincerity, honesty, and integrity increase the value of your total package because everyone wants to be with someone they can respect.

Learning to Invest and Trust. True partnership occurs when two people are willing to invest in each other's lives. Giving each other room to grow and nurture special interests without fear or jealousy will mean many long and happy years together.

I want my wife, Aladrian, to have the space and freedom to do the things that make her come alive. And she gives me that in return. However, there is an added step in this for me. I don't need Aladrian to be involved in all my interests. Most men don't need that. All she needs to do is say, "You just go and play golf with your friends, baby, and have a good time." That makes me love her all the more. But she needs a little more than my okay when it comes to her interests. She needs my involvement. I don't have to go to the salon with her and her girlfriends to get a pedicure, but I know she loves to do that so I do things to make it possible. Guys, here are some ideas:

- Surprise her and her friends with a gift certificate to go to a spa for a day or a weekend.
- Offer to handle some errands so she has time to go.
- Even if all you can do is suggest to her that she make a trip there, she'll appreciate your thoughtfulness.

Little things like that let her know you want to invest in the things that bring her joy. To Aladrian those little things are very big things. And she doesn't forget them.

If your man wants to go back to school, encourage him. If your woman wants to get in better shape, work out with her. If he needs some quiet time, check out for a few days and leave him alone. Listen to her dreams and help her plan her future in a way that includes making those dreams a reality.

You both will feel adored by each other, and it's so little effort on your part. This is a perfect example of how you pour the kind of love someone else needs into them without any thought of what you'll get in return.

Giving each other room, believe it or not, also means you don't have to describe every conversation you have with your best girlfriend, and he doesn't have to share every moment of the time he spent with his buddies last weekend. Part of what makes people unique is their little secrets and the little things that bring them joy.

Aladrian doesn't take it personally that I share a lot of activities with friends, family, and coworkers that don't, and never will, involve her. She has a life that is separate from me in that way too. It's not dishonest or unloving for us to keep certain things from each other. We have an "us" and we still preserve the "me" in each of us.

Here are a few simple ground rules:

- Don't snoop or pry in his private affairs. If he wants you to know something, he'll tell you.
- Don't sneak a peak at her journal.
- Don't run a credit check behind his back.
- Stay out of dresser drawers, file cabinets, and e-mails.
- Don't go around and ask his friends about things you doubt about him. Go directly to him with those concerns.
- Don't tell her who her friends can be or bad-mouth her girlfriends when you're mad about something.

If you're reading this and saying, "I've done that!" then you're acting out of fear and that will only lead to failure of the relationship. Even though you should trust each other on a basic level until one of you gives the other a reason *not* to trust, there remains a much deeper level of trust that must be earned. When the time is right, your partner will let you in to more private places of his or her life. Until then, learn to live with the fact that there may always be some places you will never have access.

Learning to Take Care of Business. There is a fine line in relationships when it comes to taking care of business. And there are several areas to address here.

The Body. This is the inevitable place where we talk about first attractions. It's true that men are visually stimulated. Our eyes are powerful sex organs! When we see a woman across a crowded room and she has that certain something—beautiful hair, sexy eyes, curves that need a danger sign, or a laugh that makes our toes tingle—we'll approach her in an effort to get to know her.

But hold on, ladies! Before you say, "I know what men are looking for, and I'm never going to be a Victoria's Secret model!" let me tell you that love looks like many things to a man. Style, grace, and sensuality come in all shapes and sizes. And when beauty speaks, we listen.

We'll cross the room to search out the inner beauty of a woman (patience, kindness, grace, honesty, strength, sense of humor, and most importantly, her responsiveness to us) if we first see something on the outside that catches our eye—and that could be as simple as a great smile, a twinkle in the eye, or ladylike poise in the face of pressure.

> *A man falls in love through his eyes,*
> *a woman through her ears.*
>
> Woodrow Wyatt

We all should give careful attention to our bodies, fitness, hair, skin, and clothes—not just for the sake of attracting someone, but for ourselves. We want to be healthy and balanced in all areas without living in bondage to anything. That means we don't have to spend all our time at the gym or visiting plastic surgeons to achieve some unreachable standard of perfection.

One of the chief complaints I hear from married couples is that "she let herself go" or "he sat in the recliner, watched TV, and grew a beer gut." Don't be one of those people who keep it all together until you get your spouse and then stop trying to look good. Saying "I do" means "I'll keep doing it!"

Lewis says:

I love the way Arletta takes care of herself. She's poised and lovely and gracious. But more than that, she understands how important her *security* is to me. I'd move heaven and earth to make her feel safe, but I need to know that if something happens to me and I can't be around to take care of things, she'll be okay handling affairs on her own.

I'm in the military and travel a lot with my work, so I'm gone for long periods of time. Arletta knows how demanding my work is, and she knows I can't worry about her every second of the day. Because she is so strong, independent, and capable in my absence, I can count on her and focus on succeeding at my daily tasks.

Some of the guys in my unit are dating some real drama queens. They are so whiney and helpless when they're on the road—not Arletta. She nourishes me. She nourishes my idea of true partnership.

Hero vs. Villain. Another area of taking care of business is knowing when *not* to take care of business. For instance, as much as we men would like to think women can't deal with life without us, we're adding too much pressure to our own lives, and we're not giving her enough credit. We don't have to carry every burden, fix every problem, fight every battle, remove every obstacle, or carry her across any finish line. Women know struggle builds character.

Dr. Ronn

Fixing Things

Aladrian knows I'm right there beside her in the face of adversity, not running ahead of her to make sure the coast is clear. I'm giving myself a little more room to breathe and, most importantly, blessing Aladrian's life by lifting her up and encouraging her.

When Aladrian has a conflict at work or with family, I don't go Tank Boy on her, insist on taking over, and flatten the situation. I let her know I'm there to bounce around ideas about how to handle the conflict. I talk to her about it without going commando. If she's confused about something and can't make a decision, I don't make the decision for her. I give her my two cents' worth if she asks for it. Otherwise, I just let her know I'm there to help if she needs it, and I stand back.

When she's down and feeling bad about something, I don't put on the proverbial red cape and try to save the day. Sometimes she doesn't want the day to be saved. Sometimes she just needs to feel down about it. Everybody feels bad sometimes. As much as I love her and want to help, I have trained myself to just sit with her and let her know I'm there.

Hey, my first inclination is always to strap on my tool belt and fix every broken thing. I fight the urge every day to divide and conquer every one of Aladrian's problems. But lots of mistakes and lots of time have taught me to set the tool belt where we both can see it—the security is visible to her—but I wait in the wings for my cue. Oh, I have plenty of opportunities to be heroic Mr. Tool Man to Aladrian. But moving in before my cue just makes me Mr. Annoying Buttinsky, and that makes me a curse rather than a blessing to my wife.

One of the most valuable lessons I've learned is that good intentions can be easily misinterpreted. You may be trying to fix a *problem*, but your partner may see you trying to fix *him* or *her*.

Time. Those who manage their time well know they have to set priorities. Your number one priority should always be your relationship with God. Everything you do will follow the pattern of your relationship with God. You can't spend all your free time at church. That's not balance. Likewise, you can't spend all your free time working. You have to find a way to do your work but then leave it at the office.

When you're on a date, give your date your undivided attention (and that means turn the cell phone off!). Or at the very least, give your attention to whatever it is you're doing together. When I was dating Aladrian, she always knew when my mind was somewhere else, and even though she didn't always mention it, I know it hurt her if I wasn't focused on the event at hand.

Find the balance in your life filled with church, work, love, family, friends, and time to be alone. We're going to talk about this in greater detail in chapter ten.

Money. Another important matter to take care of relates to the most obvious—money. Everyone has heard the old axiom, "A fool and his money are soon parted." Some of us have an uncanny ability to spot that fool a mile away, and too many women today have felt the sting of having to take care of this bit of business in a relationship. Sometimes women are forced to carry the financial burden completely. Women are capable of surviving in ways that baffle me. I have counseled many women who don't mind being given that responsibility—when it's absolutely necessary. And they don't mind sharing the financial burdens in a relationship. But they do mind being taken advantage of because they can manage money and their men can't. It's not right and it's not fair that men should put that kind of burden on women.

Here is some solid advice about taking care of financial business for both men and women in a dating relationship:

- If you're having trouble managing your finances, there are resources to help you. Sign up for a Financial Peace[10] class and learn how to budget and pay off your debts. You should do this before you get married. You should consider doing this before you even start dating.

- Think early about how your present financial situation is going to be broached with your future partner. Being in a dating relationship doesn't mean you get to see the other person's bank statements or credit report. But it does mean you're going to have to come clean about your finances at some point. You definitely don't want to have to tell your mate you have eight credit cards maxed out, and your utilities are always being turned off due to nonpayment.

- Don't ask your partner to help you with your rent (especially if you just got back from a weekend in Vegas).

- Don't spend a lot of money on toys for yourself and then buy a cheap gift for your partner's birthday. That's just rude.

- When you both decide to date each other on an exclusive basis, you should have the money talk. You should discuss how you handle your money now, and then decide how to continue managing your money.

- If you start talking about marriage, you'll need to make more decisions about how money is managed and what happens when it stops being *your* money and *my* money and it becomes *our* money.

Don't ignore this important aspect of your package! Problems that arise because you don't have a solid financial philosophy will not go away, and you can't ignore them. Spend a little, save a little, give a little away, and don't forget to tithe. Together make this a priority in your relationship.

Learning the Value of Faithfulness. Everyone wants to find a relationship with a person who is open, honest, and faithful. But sadly, few people actually find those three qualities in one person. We live in a cursed world, one that teaches us it's easier to lie to get what we want. Our sin nature whispers to us, "It's okay to cheat. No one will know." And it's true that, sometimes, no one will find out. If we only knew *which* times we'd get caught with our pants down, it sure would be easier to plan our cheating, right? Wrong!

The problem is that being dishonest and unfaithful aren't things that develop naturally in Christian men and women. We don't set out, plot, or plan to cheat in our relationships. We don't deliberately set out to hurt, lie, or shut our partner out.

Dr. Ronn

Faithfulness

This is what I've learned from counseling individuals who have been unfaithful: There is always a precipitating action or event that sets the pendulum swinging. Then before long, they're swinging out of control, and most of the time that precipitating action or event doesn't have anything to do with their partner.

But I've also counseled those who faced temptation and chose the correct path to faithfulness and honesty. They were able to open up and share their deepest thoughts with their partners. Still, I know that as long as sin lives in this world, there will be folks who aren't faithful or honest.

So how do those who can resist the urge and temptation do it? Are they made of steel? Do they have some secret mantra they recite when faced with the tough decisions? Do they have some extra thing in their DNA that makes them stronger?

No, that's not it. In fact, if we can conceive of it in our hearts, then we are capable of doing it. Humans are capable of all sorts of monstrous things. We read about these horrific acts in the paper every day—murder, rape, war, pornography, drugs, abandonment, child abuse, bigamy, tax evasion, embezzlement...the list goes on and on. So again, how do the faithful ones keep from doing these terrible things?

I have only one explanation: the grace of God. The grace of God makes us tender, not weak. The grace of God can reach into our souls and set us on the right course, like an internal compass pointing due heaven. The grace of God shows us that the long road home to the Father's house is actually a very short path. How successfully we travel that path depends on how much we depend on Christ for our strength and how much we view Him as the true Light of our lives.

Those we choose to walk with desperately need us to follow Christ. They need to know that the grace of God lives in us and guides us, and that when we're faced with the tough decisions, they're not really so tough—we know the right thing to do and we just do it.

Your partner needs to know you will be faithful and honest—and not just with him or her. Your partner wants to know that you would be faithful to anyone you were with. He or she wants to know you are honest because it's right to be honest.

If you are in a relationship right now that's damaged because you've been dishonest, unfaithful, or not forthcoming with your true feelings, it's not beyond repair. Again, the grace of God can work miracles in a relationship. If both of you are willing to work at it and bring every dark thing to light, confess it, ask forgiveness from God and each other, and leave it in the past, then there is no end to the healing that can take place in your lives together.

Learning to Pray Together. There are few things that make a man feel loved more than a woman praying for him. And a woman feels closer and more secure if she knows her man is praying for her. But don't just pray for each other in your bedtime prayers; wrap your hands together and spend some time on your knees before the Lord as a couple.

You increase the value of your package when you show your mate you are willing to go to the mat to appeal to God for strength, courage, patience, forgiveness, and love. The best relationships occur when a couple makes time together to ask God how they can better serve Him. Praying with your partner is the concrete foundation of the house you build together in God's kingdom.

> *If a man wishes to be sure of the road he treads on,*
> *he must close his eyes and walk in the dark.*
>
> ST. JOHN OF THE CROSS

Learning to Celebrate Victories and Accept Failures. Although only one runner in the Boston Marathon can come in first place, all who finish the race worked just as hard as that one runner who crossed the finish line first.

Dr. Ronn

Failure

Failure is an inevitable part of every relationship. Your partner will eventually disappoint you in some way, and you will do the same to him or her. When you leave the door open for each other to stumble without fear of rejection, it's much easier to recover. There is a Japanese proverb that goes, "Fall down six times, get up seven." You will *always* fall, but the point is to keep getting up.

Let your partner know it's okay to fall, and let him or her know you'll be there for support when it's time to get up again. The essence of true partnership lies in allowing your partner to carry you when you're too tired to walk on your own and returning that loving gesture when he or she is faced with failure.

Learning to Curb Expectations. The hardest part of living life is accepting the realities we encounter.

===== *Amanda says:* =====

Clay treats me like a candidate for an extreme makeover reality show. He's a compulsive controller who thinks he's in my life for the sole purpose of making me into his "ideal" woman.

He's always ready with his unsolicited advice, not-so-helpful tips on how to improve myself, and ways I can make more money and be more successful. He tells me who my friends should be based on how much they can help me succeed. The worst part is that he can't respond to me romantically if my standards for the day aren't up to par for him. He doesn't feel like my boyfriend—he feels like my drill sergeant! He has completely unrealistic expectations of me. You know…I'm going to go and get a dog at the local animal shelter. At least it will appreciate me!

It's normal to have a picture in your mind of who you think is perfect for you; however, your "perfect" partner is in fact going to be far from perfect. When approaching relationships, you have to understand these average baseline opinions about the opposite sex:

- People in relationships are at their best when they are *confident* that their relationship is solid, filled with devotion, faithfulness, and consistency.

- People have almost limitless love, encouragement, and affection for their partner when they are *secure* in their partner's love for them.

- People must be able to *depend* on their partner for the steady supply of their best treasure—their partner's sincere and demonstrated devotion and commitment to them.

You'll notice that the common denominators here are confidence, security, and dependability. Your need for these things can easily be misinterpreted as a need to see your partner perform better. The internal driving force for all of us is fueled by our pursuit of an overall sense of security (stability, harmony, and intimacy).

Dr. Ronn

Trophies

Don't get me wrong, men, a woman loves knowing her man is proud of her, and she loves it when he shows it in front of other people—to a degree. But when you turn her into a *thing* instead of the woman she is, you weaken and cheapen her. You've pulled a strong woman from the ranks of strong women throughout time, and you've stripped her naked in front of the entire world.

You know how it feels, don't you? At least once in your life, you were held to an impossibly high standard by someone—your father, your mother, a teacher, a coach, maybe even a girlfriend or a wife. When you realize you cannot live up to that random heroic image to earn and keep the love of another person, it robs you of your strength. It strips you of your masculinity.

The same holds true for the woman you love. Her feminine strength is a tightly woven garment that holds together her charms, her mystique, her spirituality, her personality, and her love for you. It also holds the promise of her future, the children she might bear with you, the adversities she will face.

Do not weaken this woman with your impossible expectations and your glory-seeking grandstanding. You need this woman strong. You never know when you'll have to call on that strength to help you stand. Also, you'll want her to teach that strength to her children—your children.

The reality is that it's not about performance or failure to perform. Life itself is not perfect. Your partner needs to know (and you need to be assured of the same from your partner) that the ground may shake, but you're not going to fall through a crack and disappear on him or her. You don't have to be their kingdom come. Just let your heart be their home.

Joy's Story
WAITING FOR MR. PERFECT

Joy is thirty-two years old, highly successful in her medical field, beautiful, funny, intelligent, and still single. To be honest, she has only been on two dates in the past ten years. The problem? She's waiting for Mr. Perfect.

"It's not that I'm dismissing opportunities," Joy says. "I just know my eternally fine, brilliant, highly spiritual, honest, outspoken, ambitious, self-reliant, passionate and sexually proficient, nurturing, intuitive, perfect blend of extroverted and introverted picture of flawlessness is out there somewhere. I don't want to be wasting my time with Mr. Almost Perfect and miss my chance with Mr. Perfect!"

"Joy, do you think it's possible that the man with all those qualities walked by you eight times yesterday, and you didn't notice because he wasn't packaged in the way you fantasized?"

"No way," she says, "I would have noticed."

Learning the Art of Romance. No matter what you've been taught about men always having to be the initiator of romance, know this: Romance is a two-way street, and learning how to travel this road is a great way to package yourself for success.

Yes, traditionally, men have been the ones to send the flowers and the cards, buy the dinners and the jewelry, and plan the romantic dates. It's true! We take a lot of pride in these things. So why would we want our women stealing our thunder? Because we love having it done for us! Why else would we spend so much time doing these things for our women?

Dr. Ronn

Romance

Every time I give Aladrian flowers or treat her to a candle-light dinner, she sees the soft underbelly of my heart. I do these things for her because of the delight I see in her eyes. I'm always rewarded for that effort with her soft, fluttering kisses and sweet words of appreciation.

Imagine my surprise when I found out Aladrian had been watching me closely, and figuring out what made my heart come alive—what made my eyes light up, what made me grab her and tell her she is the most wonderful woman alive. And then she started romancing me with those things!

There is absolutely no doubt that learning the art of romance will increase the value of your total package, but I want to be clear about this: Among married couples who love each other, romance and physical affection don't always have to lead to sex.

I'm sure you've heard the popular myth that women don't like sex as much as men. Well, it's a myth because it's simply not true. Before you walk down the aisle, you need to know that the real issue is not a like or dislike of sex, it is how each gender approaches "making love."

Remember that a man's most powerful sex organ is his eyes. He can see a woman and become aroused. Most of the time, ladies, the only way your future husbands will be able to see that arousal through to completion is to engage in the physical act of sex. This, of course, isn't true of all men, but be prepared in the event it's true of your man.

For a woman sex involves *all* her senses, and she doesn't have to have sexual intercourse to see her arousal through to completion. Long before a sexual act takes place and long after, a woman is creating and re-creating the act of love in her mind.

Women tend to become suspicious of love play if it always turns into foreplay. So, potential husbands, it's best to make sure that every physical act of love doesn't turn into sex. Be affectionate with her, hold her hand, caress and embrace her, cuddle her, and talk to her. This is love talk to a woman. It may not always lead to the act of making love, but you will be making a special kind of love to her just the same—a love that she relates to, and a love that makes her love you more and more. This is all very simple to understand! So learn it before you say "I do"!

Dr. Ronn

Sex

In case some of you men still have doubts about this fact, let me just enlighten you: Women aren't like us! We see it and our bodies immediately engage. You can't engage a woman's body without first engaging her mind and her heart. Put simply, we men are a one-step operation. Women are a multiple-step operation.

A woman can see a sexy, half-dressed man and not want to jump into bed with him. She may admire his physique, his eyes, his hair, what little clothes he may be wearing, and the way he carries himself. But admiration and appreciation may be as far as it goes for her.

If that same sexy man spends time with her, talks to her, listens to her, engages in the things that bring her joy, takes care of her heart, invests his time and energy in her, makes her feel treasured and loved, and says her name in that oh-so-special way—well, the multiple steps of operation are a lot easier to engage.

I could literally go on for many more pages about the romance issue because every person is different and every need changes from month to month and day to day—sometimes hour to hour. It must be the adventurer in us that makes that winding, nebulous path so inviting and irresistible. It's the mystery of it that invites you in, and it's your mastery of it that completes your package.

What's Next?

We've run the gamut in this chapter, haven't we? You've learned that what the world sees is what a potential date will see—it's your product, what you have to share with any companion or potential partner. You've learned that your core values shape your product, and that diving into the depths of the other-centered world is where you get the knowledge to be a better, more dateable person.

Remember, you're in control of how you package yourself, how much you learn about the opposite sex, and how you let that knowledge shape who you are.

Now, I think we should spend some time learning how to market yourself. Remember when your mama said to always put your best foot forward? Well, she was right!

CHAPTER FIVE

Zippers & Flush Toilets

For centuries people in business have poured their lives and creativity into something they've believed in, something they've had faith in—a product or a service they had believed was so special that they wanted to share it with the world. Today those who care enough about their products spare no expense in developing a way to show the world just how wonderful they are. They spend time creating ways to show—or market—the best assets of their products. They research all possible markets (potential buyers) to find out who would benefit the most from them. And when they feel they are ready to release their wonderful products to the world, they dive in with great hopes and expectations.

When you stop to think about it, doesn't dating follow the same kind of action plan? Yes, I understand there may be some hesitation on your part to accept the idea of strategically marketing yourself in the area of relationships. After all, the term *marketing* sounds so cold and impersonal. But that's really the essence of what you're doing when you decide to step out there and start dating. If this is a foreign concept to you, I just ask that you trust me while you read through this book. I promise that the benefits will outweigh and ultimately banish your hesitation.

So how do you go about preparing yourself for the world? Well, in chapter three you determined specifically who you wanted to share your life with by narrowing down your market. What's more, you discovered something about yourself. You made the wise decision that you are very special and that somewhere out there is a person who would find great value in you. You know you have something special to show the world. The next step is learning how to show it.

The work ahead of us won't be simple, so you're going to have to take up a spirit of adventure and trust. Dating with an eye to recognize your soul mate isn't always easy or pleasant—in fact, sometimes it's downright hard and even heartbreaking—but that doesn't mean you shouldn't try. We would never have benefited from the great ideas of others if they'd given up letting the world know about their great products. Where would we be if Mr. Whitcomb Judson thought the zipper was a dumb idea? What would have happened if Tim Berners-Lee was laughed out of every room because of his dream that became the Internet! And there is a heated debate about who invented the flush toilet, but who cares who came up with that idea! Someone obviously thought it was a good one, and I, for one, am glad that person put a lot of effort into letting the world know about it.

I'm not comparing you to zippers and flush toilets. I'm just saying that bringing two hearts together is so much more important than man bringing zippers and flush toilets to the world. I know this because joining hearts and lives is my passion in life, and that's why I'm sharing it with you.

So you see, when you're passionate about that thing inside you, something you cherish and believe in, and you want to share that thing with the world, you have to put some effort into revealing it. Folks aren't just going to show up on your doorstep and say, "Hey, I hear you have something special!" The world will never know about you if you don't show them who you are and what you have. That's why you have to package and market yourself. Only then will someone look at you and say, "Yes, that is what I've been looking for!"

Market Yourself

So they said to him, "What did He do to you? How did
He open your eyes?"

JOHN 9:26 NASB

✁

One of the quickest ways to end a relationship with a man is to start playing games with his head or his heart. Hidden agendas can stay hidden for only so long before they come to light. After that, you better be prepared for a showdown. Games make a man feel "played," and that can make him feel stupid. And stupid is the last thing a man wants to be. Laura is going to find this out the hard way.

I'm in my fourth counseling session with Laura, and today is the day that I tell her she can't use her sexuality to drive up the stakes in her play for what she wants. She dresses conservatively at church, but when she goes to work and out on dates, she dresses suggestively and gives little care as to what she says or how she behaves in the presence of men. Likewise, based on what she's told me, she's been playing money and power games with her boyfriend.

I know she's ready to hear the truth, so I ask her, "Laura, have you ever heard of that common fraudulent marketing practice known as 'bait and switch,' where customers are lured by false advertising into purchasing something they think has great value and can get with very little effort? In reality the seller has no intention of ever offering the advertised high quality product. After the deal is sealed, it is revealed to the customer that what they purchased isn't *available anymore (it was never actually available), but a substitute is."*

"Yes, I've heard of that. I guess you're saying that's what I'm doing with Steven."

"Well, you've been dating him for about two months and from what you've told me, that's exactly what you've done. You're also doing it with Brandon, Mark, and Jerry. I do appreciate your candor, and I hope you can appreciate mine in return."

"It's okay. I really hate the way I am," she whispers, "but it's the only way I know how to be."

"Do you want to learn a new way?" I ask her.

"Yes." She looks me in the eye and firmly replies, "I do."

Over the course of the next couple of months, I teach Laura another common marketing practice known as branding. Branding is a way of collecting all the information about a product and packaging it in a way that reveals all the information in one great effort. She agrees to see a stylist about settling on a personal style that is conservative but enhances her natural beauty. She agrees that her behavior and dress should always be the same, whether she's in church, at work, or on a date. Best of all, Laura agrees that branding is exactly what she needs to let men know the whole truth about her amazing product—that she's a wonderful, godly woman who wants to be treated with respect in a mutually exclusive relationship with a man she can honor.

In my last session with Laura, she is so put together and sharp. She has decided she doesn't want to date anyone for a while. She just wants to get to know herself a little better and take some night classes.

Laura is a perfect example of a woman who learned the value of packaging and marketing her product the proper *way. She removed guilt, control, manipulation, and game-playing from her relationships and is now giving herself a chance to rest before establishing a strong and honest relationship with a man. "When the time is right," she says, "I'm going to honestly expose my goals and objectives, and let him know he's made an intelligent choice by choosing me."*

An important part of a good marketing plan is examining the internal factors of a product (and remember, that's you) to determine if it's ready to be turned loose on the market. No one is perfect, and you've learned that you don't have to be perfect to be a blessing to someone. But by working through all the things you needed to learn—love and respect, criticism and applause, sharing yourself, being faithful, speaking the universal language of love, learning to trust, paying attention to detail, even how to fight fair—you've successfully arrived at the next step: examining the *external* factors of relationship marketing in order to get a grip on how you want to start marketing yourself.

There are many important external factors to consider, but the great news is that all those factors are encapsulated into one unit: a man or a woman. Before you start thinking, *Good! This should be easy,* you should know it's not going to be that simple. In fact the quest of trying to figure out how to market yourself to the opposite sex is an endless and sometimes painful pursuit. Some people describe it as trying to teach a pig to sing. They say it wastes your time and annoys the pig.

The difference here, of course, is that it's not a waste of time at all—it's probably some of the most important time you'll ever spend.

The Basic Marketing Plan

Putting together a marketing strategy was the first step in the successful marketing model. In chapter three you did just that. By thoroughly researching your market for a very specific snapshot of who you're interested in pursuing, you not only helped develop your own product, but you have a clear idea of how to position yourself in the market. In chapter four you worked on the product. You prayed and meditated, you took an honest, hard look at issues you may have had, and now you're confident you have a product that's worth marketing. So what's next?

Well, you need to make marketing mix decisions—a process that is all about you! You must decide how you want the world to see and interpret you. It's all about your signature style, personality, likes and dislikes, spiritual, emotional, and physical health, behaviors, beliefs, and core values. How you put all these factors together gives the world a snapshot of you. It's what the market will see at first glance. You determine what and how much it will see. Call it your "promotional package," if you will.

As time goes on—as you implement your marketing strategy—you'll continue to exercise control, which simply means periodically monitoring the environment for changing conditions and trends and making adjustments to your marketing mix to suit those changing conditions. You must learn to adapt and change with shifting environments. Sometimes it's necessary to pull back and redesign your product and your strategy to get the best results. It's a continual monitoring and adaptation process, but well worth the effort because it'll keep you on the cutting edge of a changing market for as long as your product is out there.

Package and Repackage Your Product

We all say we want somebody who will love us the way we are. Until you find that person, figure out the best ways to accentuate your strengths (not that you should stop accentuating your strengths once you've found your one and only). You'll have to try a lot of different ways to market yourself. Try something different for a month or two. Then revise your package. Find out the best way to compensate for or minimize your flaws and try it out.

How do you know how to package yourself? Women often get together with their girlfriends and ask one another, "What do you think of this? Does this look good?" Ladies, your women friends might agree with you, but women are not your market. A better way of finding the truth is to ask those questions of your male friends who aren't interested in you romantically. They are more typical of your market. The same works for you men. You'll need a discerning eye so ask women friends or coworkers for their honest opinions…not your basketball buddies.

Find out not only what is available, but what's possible. Don't wait for the *Extreme Makeover* crew to show up at your door unannounced. Take advantage of what is available to you now. Put yourself in a new package and see how it works. Nothing ventured, nothing gained! If you invest some time in packaging and repacking your product, you'll be happier with yourself, and a potential mate will be happy with you too.

Because you want to package yourself as someone who's worth getting to know, here are some ideas to help you get started:

- Read novels and biographies of famous people. Do things that enhance your knowledge and exposure. You might be a wonderful person but not able to hold a conversation for very long because you aren't up to speed on current events or history. Become a more interesting person.

- Ask people who have excellent taste and who reflect some of the qualities you're looking for in a potential mate for ideas on how to package yourself.

- Find people who will challenge you. Give yourself a little freedom to be different.

- Improve your vocabulary.

- Take a class on etiquette.

- Read popular magazines.

- Start to notice other people—what they're wearing, what they're talking about, and what they do.

- Check out the Internet for ideas.

- Travel—it expands your horizons, gives you some great stories, and you might even meet someone along the way.

A Blue Chip Brand

Remember the lesson Laura had to learn: Don't bait and switch in an effort to attract a man's attention. Let him know exactly what he's getting by using another common marketing practice—branding. As I said earlier, it may sound funny, but branding is a way of collecting all the information about a product or service and packaging it in a way that reveals it all in one great effort. Successful branding includes a logo (your individual personality), images, color schemes, and symbols (your individual style). Branding works when it's honest and it tells the whole truth about an amazing product.

You are the product. If you brand yourself properly and honestly, the inevitable result will be yet another common marketing phenomenon known as "brand recognition" wherein you become widely known in the marketplace by a strong, positive sentiment. A person will develop a strong sense of loyalty to what he or she views as "brand equity," which is the value placed on the brand and what someone is willing to invest in it to seek exclusive proprietary rights.

Remember that a true market is based on freedom—freedom to choose and to act on those choices. Guilt, manipulation, and game-playing effectively shut down the market and any chance you have of establishing a strong and honest relationship with someone special. Expose all your goals and objectives to your partner. Make that person feel he or she made an intelligent choice by choosing to be with you.

What's Next?

Hopefully, by now you're beginning to believe that experiencing the love of your life *IS* absolutely possible! But merely *believing* is never enough—any more than faith without works is enough. Real faith means you can count on God to do His part and that God can count on you to do yours.

So, are you ready to take bold, new action in order to experience something new and improved in your love life? I hope you are. If so, take a long deep breath and turn the page. You are about to encounter the essence of my *No-Nonsense Dating* message. And, believe me, you *can* do this!

CHAPTER SIX

Worth the *Wait* of Diamonds

You'd be surprised at the places you can find diamonds these days. Depending on the quality you're seeking, you can find them just about anywhere—including a discount store!

If you walk into that discount store looking for a diamond, they'll make it affordable for you. You might even be able to put it on layaway and have an easy payment plan. It will be a diamond that didn't cost you very much, but it will still be a diamond.

However, if you want a superior quality diamond that has great value on the market, you'll fly to Beverly Hills and go to Tiffany & Co. They sell diamonds too, but you'll likely receive a disapproving look if you mention the word *layaway*. If you have to ask, "How much?" you probably can't afford it. And don't wait for the clearance sale. They don't have one.

A diamond from Tiffany's will be costly, in dollars and in the time spent pursuing it. But once you've fooled around with the discount store diamonds, you realize there is a lot more riding on the Tiffany diamond than just the time and money. It's worth every inconvenience, struggle, risk, and investment. That Tiffany diamond is so beautiful, so precious, so unique, you forget the pain of obtaining it.

You see where I'm going with this and how it translates to relationships. You can spend all the time and money in the world on those low-quality relationships, but when you realize there is a relationship out there that is so beautiful, so precious, and so unique for you, you're no longer interested in constantly choosing the lesser of two evils, or for that matter, the lesser of *several* evils and then afterward, regretfully counting the cost. It's okay to admit you're ready to lay it down and have the best.

I've got great news for you. Potential partners have something else in common with Tiffany diamonds: There are a lot of exceptionally high-quality ones out there. Until you find the one who captures your heart, you can take your time, browse, and try some on! The best one is somewhere waiting for you. You just need to know where to be to see and be seen by that special one.

Now, let's find out about where to show up, and how to get in the game.

6

Show Up—And Get In the Game

*The kingdom of heaven is like treasure hidden in a field,
which a man found and hid; and for joy over it he goes
and sells all that he has and buys that field. Again, the
kingdom of heaven is like a merchant seeking beautiful pearls, who, when he had found one pearl of great
price, went and sold all that he had and bought it.*

MATTHEW 13:44-46

❧

*Janise has her mind made up. She is not going to make any
effort to find the one.*

"No," *she says,* "my grandmother made it very clear to
me that I cannot look for my future husband. He'll find
me. And when he does, God will reveal to me that he's the
one."

"Why do you think that?" *I ask, even though I have an
inkling of what she might say next.*

"Proverbs eighteen…"

"Twenty-two," *I say finishing her response.* "Yes, I hear
it all the time."

"Well, then you understand," *she states relieved.*

"Janise, things get weird when we start requiring God
to speak a name to us. Is that how God reveals His will to
you? He is certainly capable of revealing His will in that
manner, but He gave us His Word—the Bible—to guide
us in life matters. He gave us the gift of free will—the ability to choose—so that we could make decisions for ourselves
with His blessing."

"I'm not sure I believe that," Janise said. "But I think I want to believe it."

"Janise, if God hadn't given you free will and if He made all your decisions for you, I could understand what you've believed all this time. But if that were true, you'd have no part of any day-to-day decisions—neither the complicated ones nor the mundane ones."

Janise is completely taken aback. "Look," I tell her, "I know your grandmother meant well with her teachings, but if you can recognize free will as a gift and a blessing from God, and if you can appreciate the good mind He put inside you, then you have to allow for the possibility that God wants you to exercise that free will and use that sharp mind to partner with Him to do His work in your life…and probably make some mistakes but learn from them."

"I can't believe you're actually telling me it's okay for me to date." Janise is smiling now. "I didn't expect that!"

"Not only am I telling you it's okay to date, but it's okay for you to actively market yourself as an eligible, single woman. Janise, I have the experience and the authority to speak this truth to you. Now let's talk about where some of your best opportunities are."

Implementing an action plan for your dating life includes knowing *where* you need to be for the most successful exposure. Woody Allen rightly observed that 90 percent of life is just showing up! Your wonderfully packaged product doesn't do you a bit of good if it's just sitting at home eating Dove bars. Showing up is the point at which you take the leap of faith and put yourself out there.

Truth in the Parables

In our opening verses for this chapter, you'll find two parables Jesus shared with His followers. In Matthew 13:44, the parable of the hidden treasure, notice the man has accidentally discovered a treasure, and he takes steps to secure it. In verses 45-46, the parable of the pearl of great price, the man goes out and deliberately seeks the best pearl, and when he finds it, he does what is necessary for him to secure it.

The lesson in these parables is that there are *two* ways to go about obtaining a treasure; you can stumble onto it by accident, or you can make a very deliberate and concerted effort to get it. Put in context for today, which treasure would you be most proud of? I'd say the one you worked hard and made a calculated effort to acquire. You place a higher value on something when you invest more of yourself.

Let's consider the intentional act of visiting the places and investing yourself where you're likely to find your treasure. You may be thinking, *Hold on a second! This is moving too fast! I'm not ready!* Yes, you are ready. In the previous steps, you decided what you want and who you're looking for. You also decided what you want the world to see when they get to know you. Step three is the necessary *launch*—the scary and exciting process of putting yourself in strategic places with a strategic plan. Before you know it, you'll be dealing with crowd control, which is a very good thing (even if it sounds a little overwhelming right now).

Dr. Ronn

Recklessness

I have to say this because if I don't, someday someone is going to show up at the pearly gates ready to receive applause and a reward from God for doing something… dumb. That's right. I don't want you to stand there and say, "But this man wrote a book and told me I should take risks, so I went to all these bad places and got into all these stupid relationships. Sure it was foolish, but I was just doing what the man told me to do!"

Don't even think about doing that! I don't want to hear you ever say, "I don't understand! Those crazy people I got involved with just snatched my heart out of my chest, threw it on the ground, put their cigarettes out on it, and then stomped on it again! What happened?"

I'll tell you what happened: That wasn't faith. That was foolishness, and you get absolutely no credit for reckless behavior. Showing up at *strategic* places with a *strategic* plan is your insurance policy against total destruction. Yes, sharing your product with the world leaves you vulnerable. You're going to get your feelings hurt sometimes. You may have already gotten your feelings hurt in a relationship. It didn't feel good. It made you cry. It made you depressed. But now you look back and you know it would take a whole lot more to throw you to the ground like that.

Your product got tougher—it changed from vinyl into leather, plastic into steel. You don't get that kind of refinement in a laboratory. It comes from real life. And the only way to experience real life is to show up—with a plan, not with reckless abandon.

An Investment Plan Just for You

At this time, you'll need to go back and fetch the list of top five ways and opportunities to meet *the one,* which you created on page 43. By now you've had a chance to mull the list over and maybe thought of additions.

Defining What Makes You Come Alive

Imagine finding a partner who enjoys the same things you love doing. If you hate smoke-filled bars, then you wouldn't go to one to find a date. If you have allergies to animals, then you wouldn't volunteer at the local animal shelter in order to find your true love. Of course those are obvious, but I don't want you wasting any time in places where you're going to be unhappy. So let's help you narrow down where your true interests lie.

Start by making a list of the interests, hobbies, or pursuits that give you the most joy. Make sure you include things you haven't yet pursued but would like to. Try to come up with at least 15 and list them in order of importance to you (list your top choice first). Use your list of opportunities from page 43 to get started. Be reasonable and make sure all the interests, hobbies, or pursuits can actually be done.

1. _____

2. _____

3. _____

4. _____

5. _____

6. _____

7. _____

8. _____

9. _____

10. _____

11. _____

12. _____

13. _____

14. _____

15. _____

Now divide your list into three lists of five items. If you can't come up with 15 interests, then take what you have and split it evenly into three lists, remembering to keep your top five choices in your first list. Then I want you to expand each of the lists. Starting with List A, answer the questions in the space provided. Do the same for Lists B and C. Complete this exercise, then continue on to the next section.

List A

1. _____

• Why does this particular interest, hobby, or pursuit bring me such joy?

• What need is being fulfilled when I participate in this?

• How does it make me feel when I get to do this?

- What would I be willing to give up in order to do this more?

- Is this something I want to continue doing after I meet my soul mate?

Opportunities [Read instructions on page 123]: _____

_____

Launch [Read instructions on page 124]: _____

_____

2. _____

- Why does this particular interest, hobby, or pursuit bring me such joy?

- What need is being fulfilled when I participate in this?

- How does it make me feel when I get to do this?

- What would I be willing to give up in order to do this more?

- Is this something I want to continue doing after I meet my soul mate?

Opportunities: _____

Launch:_____

3. _____

- Why does this particular interest, hobby, or pursuit bring me such joy?

- What need is being fulfilled when I participate in this?

- How does it make me feel when I get to do this?

- What would I be willing to give up in order to do this more?

- Is this something I want to continue doing after I meet my soul mate?

Opportunities: _____

Launch:_____

4. _____

- Why does this particular interest, hobby, or pursuit bring me such joy?

- What need is being fulfilled when I participate in this?

- How does it make me feel when I get to do this?

- What would I be willing to give up in order to do this more?

- Is this something I want to continue doing after I meet my soul mate?

Opportunities: _____

Launch:_____

5. _____

- Why does this particular interest, hobby, or pursuit bring me such joy?

- What need is being fulfilled when I participate in this?

- How does it make me feel when I get to do this?

- What would I be willing to give up in order to do this more?

- Is this something I want to continue doing after I meet my soul mate?

Opportunities: _____

Launch:_____

List B

1. _____

- Why does this particular interest, hobby, or pursuit bring me such joy?

- What need is being fulfilled when I participate in this?

- How does it make me feel when I get to do this?

- What would I be willing to give up in order to do this more?

- Is this something I want to continue doing after I meet my soul mate?

Opportunities: _____

Launch:_____

2. _____

- Why does this particular interest, hobby, or pursuit bring me such joy?

- What need is being fulfilled when I participate in this?

- How does it make me feel when I get to do this?

- What would I be willing to give up in order to do this more?

- Is this something I want to continue doing after I meet my soul mate?

Opportunities: _____

Launch:_____

3. _____

- Why does this particular interest, hobby, or pursuit bring me such joy?

- What need is being fulfilled when I participate in this?

- How does it make me feel when I get to do this?

- What would I be willing to give up in order to do this more?

- Is this something I want to continue doing after I meet my soul mate?

Opportunities: _____

Launch:_____

4. _____

- Why does this particular interest, hobby, or pursuit bring me such joy?

- What need is being fulfilled when I participate in this?

- How does it make me feel when I get to do this?

- What would I be willing to give up in order to do this more?

- Is this something I want to continue doing after I meet my soul mate?

Opportunities: _____

Launch:_____

5. _____

- Why does this particular interest, hobby, or pursuit bring me such joy?

- What need is being fulfilled when I participate in this?

- How does it make me feel when I get to do this?

- What would I be willing to give up in order to do this more?

- Is this something I want to continue doing after I meet my soul mate?

Opportunities: _____

Launch:_____

List C

1. _____

- Why does this particular interest, hobby, or pursuit bring me such joy?

- What need is being fulfilled when I participate in this?

- How does it make me feel when I get to do this?

- What would I be willing to give up in order to do this more?

- Is this something I want to continue doing after I meet my soul mate?

Opportunities: _____

Launch:_____

2. _____

- Why does this particular interest, hobby, or pursuit bring me such joy?

- What need is being fulfilled when I participate in this?

- How does it make me feel when I get to do this?

- What would I be willing to give up in order to do this more?

- Is this something I want to continue doing after I meet my soul mate?

Opportunities: _____

Launch:_____

3.   _____

- Why does this particular interest, hobby, pursuit bring
  me such joy?

- What need is being fulfilled when I take part in this?

- How does it make me feel when I get to do this?

- What would I be willing to give up in order to do this
  more?

- Is this something I want to continue doing after I meet
  my soul mate?

Opportunities: _____

Launch:_____

4. _____

- Why does this particular interest, hobby, or pursuit bring me such joy?

- What need is being fulfilled when I take part in this?

- How does it make me feel when I get to do this?

- What would I be willing to give up in order to do this more?

- Is this something I want to continue doing after I meet my soul mate?

Opportunities: _____

Launch: _____

5. _____

- Why does this particular interest, hobby, or pursuit bring me such joy?

- What need is being fulfilled when I take part in this thing?

- How does it make me feel when I get to do this thing?

- What would I be willing to give up in order to do this thing more?

- Is this something I want to continue doing after I meet my soul mate?

Opportunities: _____

Launch:_____

Launching Your Opportunities

Based on your new, extensive lists of interests, hobbies, and pursuits from the previous exercise, you're now going to redefine and expand your list of opportunities from chapter three.

1. Go back to lists A, B, and C and use the space indicated to fill in some general *opportunities* or physical locations where you can actively pursue each interest. If you need help, call some friends or use the Internet to do some research. Check out these examples:

- **Interest: books**
  Opportunities: bookstores, libraries, writers' conferences

- **Interest: jazz music**
  Opportunities: jazz festivals, concert series, jazz clubs

- **Interest: children**
  Opportunities: school functions, church youth groups, community youth groups

Complete this exercise then continue on to the next section.

2. Now go back to lists A, B, and C and use the space indicated to *launch* each of the opportunities. Use the Web, make some phone calls, ask people, or do some other kind of research to find out the specific locations, times, and places each of these opportunities occur. This might take some time, so commit yourself to this exercise over the next week or so. Here are some examples:

- **Interest: books**
  Opportunities: bookstores, libraries, writer's conferences
  Launch: Barnes & Noble near my house, open until 10 P.M.; city library book club on Wednesday nights, 7 P.M.; Southwest Writers' Forum, June 20, Phoenix, AZ.

- **Interest: jazz music**
  Opportunities: jazz festivals, concert series, jazz clubs
  Launch: Sacramento Jazz Fest, first week of July; Blue Note Concert Series, Whitmore Park, April 27, May 23, June 29; F. Scott's Dinner Club, live jazz Tuesday nights, 7–11 P.M.

- **Interest: children**
  Opportunities: school functions, church youth groups, community youth programs

Launch: Big Brothers and Sisters at Liberty Middle School, volunteer office 555-5555; Fellowship Bible Church student ministries, Becky Parker, 555-5555; YMCA Youth Programs, 555-5555

Complete this exercise, and then continue on to the next section.

Dr. Ronn

Becoming Overwhelmed

The reason I asked you to break down your list of 15 items into three lists of five is so you wouldn't become overwhelmed with this step. Start with List A and work through it the best you can. If you find yourself becoming less interested or you discover the caliber of person you're looking for isn't available there, move to List B, and eventually to List C. If you have a schedule that is open to accommodate all 15, go for it! Launch as many as you can comfortably fit into your schedule.

And one more thing—feel free to revise this list as often as you like. Just as it is advantageous for you to repackage yourself as needed, you should also repackage your launch plan.

Start Your Engines!

This step is very simple. Just get out your PDA, Day-Timer, or calendar and start scheduling all the items to launch. You can launch these things alone or invite a group of friends, and let them in on your action plan.

Complete this exercise, and then continue on to the next section.

Show Up—Get in the Game

Showing up at opportune places and then participating isn't difficult. You just let your heart lead you. All the activities you find joy in doing can lead you to your soul mate. Here are some additional tips that will help you along the way:

- *So you like Bible study?* Don't spend every night at a Bible study. Add some gym time to your schedule. Tell your Bible study group what you're doing and ask them to pray for your efforts. Then take a few nights away from them and do something to advance your plans and dreams.

- *Are you a sports nut?* Don't spend all your time playing basketball, guys. You have to spend some time launching yourself into other areas. You *might* find the woman you're looking for in the midst of a bunch of sweaty, heavy-breathing hoopsters, but you'll broaden your market in leaps and bounds if you show up in other places once in a while.

- *Need to get into shape?* Work out at the gym on regular nights. When someone sees you there, it will help him or her approach you if you're there on a regular basis.

- *Want to know more about something?* Take classes. This is a great way to meet people who share your interests.

- *Got an itch to see the world?* Travel. There are lots of tour group and cruise ship packages just for singles. Or just wing it and buy a Eurail pass for a week of freestyle traveling around Europe.

==================== *Tonya says:* ====================

"I wanted to find a godly man at church so I scheduled my whole life around what was going on there. Big mistake! After a couple of weeks, I looked around and noticed there were only three males present at the Wednesday night Bible study—one was the pastor, the second had one foot in the grave and the other on a banana peel, and the third was a three-year-old with a lollipop.

I guess God was showing me that I was there for the wrong reason! Needless to say, I now have a little more variety in my schedule, and the time I spend at church is really quality time.

Tips for Women

- Join a prison ministry—not to start a romance with a prisoner—to meet some of the godly men who make up the prison ministry.
- Next time your oil needs changing, buy the oil and oil filter yourself at an automotive supply store and then take them to the garage. You might meet someone interesting at the automotive store (a lot of men shop there), and that handsome guy at the garage will be impressed!
- Go to Home Depot. And don't just shop there. Go to the workshops and learn how to do home improvement projects. Believe it or not, that's really sexy to a man.
- Attend sporting events. Get educated about sports that don't bore you to tears. You don't have to wear safety orange or

watch NASCAR if you don't want to. Maybe golf is more your style. Pick something you really enjoy.

- Walk your dog at a park where you know men jog or play sports.

Tips for Men

- Change where you get your hair cut. Pick a place where women go too.
- Do your grocery shopping at larger stores where they offer more products for women. Choose stores that have floral and video departments where women might browse. Don't be afraid to ask the women questions about which products you should buy or which movies to rent.
- If you work retail, ask for a transfer to the women's department.
- Volunteer in children's church.
- Choirs are good places to meet women.
- Take your young nieces or nephews to the playground.
- Dance studios offer classes to groups. This is a great place to meet single women, and the two of you can dance into the sunset together. It's good exercise too.

More Tips for Everyone

- Look for places men and women are equally interested in going to, but are not necessarily romantic places.
- Join clubs. Do things that you'll have consistent contact with the same people who share your interests.
- You may have a policy against dating people at work, but if not, consider the office a great place to meet people. These

are people you spend a lot of time with each day—so maybe that special person is just down the hall.

- Church, of course, is a good place to meet godly people. Just make sure this isn't your only resource.

- Frequent your local bookstore. Choose ones that stay open late. Single people know they can meet people at bookstores in the evenings, especially if they have a coffee bar.

- Volunteering is a great way to meet great people. If you're volunteering your time, it means you care about giving of yourself because volunteering is an other-centered activity.

- Bars and clubs can be fun to just hang out at when you're with your friends, but clubs can be very stressful too. Don't invest a lot of expectations in an outing on a Friday or Saturday night. Instead show up on Tuesdays when they have that trivia contest!

- Stop showing up at places where you'll see someone one time and never see them again.

- You can meet people online even though it's "buyer beware." There are several Web sites for singles that offer safe ways to communicate so you can browse prospective dates and meet them only when you're ready and you choose to do so. Two of the oldest and most reputable are Match.com and eHarmony .com. Of course, there are dangers associated with meeting people online (there are dangers associated with meeting strangers anywhere for that matter) so exercise caution and make sure you tell your friends the details: who you're meeting, where you're meeting, and when you're meeting.

- There is a new trend called "speed dating" that brings single people together in a big room for some rather interesting conversation and probably even more interesting results. As the women sit at small tables, men move from one table to the next at the sound of a bell, which rings every seven minutes. For those few minutes you get a little taste of a prospective date. What a crazy idea! But it's very successful. You're guaranteed to have a very good time if you go with some of your friends.

I've been on so many blind dates I should get a free dog.

WENDY LIEBMAN

What's Next?

Now that you know where you want to go, what do you do when you get there? Your knees might be knocking and your heart may be pounding, but now it's time to learn how to approach someone you're interested in getting to know.

But that's not all! You're also going to learn how to become a more approachable person so when your soul mate shows up on the scene, he or she will be able to look at you and know you're approachable. See you in chapter seven!

Surviving the Smackdown

You need a reality check that will free you from the first-blush-willies before you walk across the room, smile, say hello, and hand that special person your card. Your card may be accepted, you may get a hello and a smile in return, and something magical may happen. But what if it doesn't? That "what if" is the biggest reason why people never make that trek across the room.

Fear of rejection is one of the most powerful fears known to man (and woman). It's like a dream many people have. You're stepping onto a tightrope and inching precariously toward someone you want to love. You're holding your heart for balance—this is the heart you plan to give to your special someone, but it's beating so hard it's making you a little wobbly. Halfway across the rope you realize the person on the other end has turned their back on you. Fear and embarrassment keep you from turning around and going back. You'd be a fool to move forward. And so you just stand there, holding your heart (which is now jumping around like a pillowcase full of kittens), you're losing your balance, and worst of all, you're feeling pretty stupid. Finally you just fall, and that's when you wake up in a cold sweat.

To a lot of people, that dream represents every experience they have had approaching someone they're interested in. To others, the dream represents how they feel every time someone of the opposite sex approaches them. They freeze. They can't put two syllables together. It's the stuff romantic comedies are made of.

You can't successfully approach someone or be someone others successfully approach without understanding the fear behind rejection and accepting some of the reasons why you get rejected. I could tell you the person you're approaching is always as nervous about being rejected as you are, but that wouldn't make you feel any better, would it? It wouldn't make your fear of approaching them go away, and it wouldn't give you the confidence of Brad Pitt or Beyoncé.

So let's go behind the scenes to understand the chemistry of what is happening inside of you before you approach someone, before you're being approached by someone, and how you can master both.

That stroll across the room (without tripping over your Kenneth Coles), that card you hand someone (which fortunately turns out to be your own and not your therapist's), that smile you offer (the one without radicchio between your teeth), and those first words you utter (the words that don't sound like an ancient language recently discovered by archaeologists) don't have to be part of your worst nightmare. Wake up! It's time to leap fearlessly from the tightrope and learn the truth about approaching and being approached.

Approach and Be Approachable

Has anyone by fussing in front of the mirror ever
gotten taller by so much as an inch?

Matthew 6:27 msg

✦

Stuart is in a rut. The last four women he introduced himself
to flattened him like a tire with a nail in it. But he has an
idea. "Hey, have you seen the movie Hitch? *I wonder if there*
is really someone like that out there; someone who can help
me get the woman I want," he says.

"Yeah, I love that movie!" I say. "But here's the thing,
Stuart—the guys in that movie already had the women of
their dreams picked out. You don't have your eye on one
particular woman. You've just sort of been shooting with
buckshot, trying to hit anything that moves."

"True. True," he says, "but not anymore. I keep getting
the slam dunk. In fact, I saw three women last week that I
really wanted to talk to, but because the last four didn't get
past 'hello' I didn't even bother."

"Stuart, do you know why those four women brushed
you off?"

"I guess I wasn't their type."

"That would be impossible to know at hello," I tell him.
"Maybe you're worrying too much and too soon about results.
What you should be focusing on is why she isn't interested at
that very moment. You know, when my kids were teenagers,
they always seemed to ask me for things at the wrong time. If
they had stopped to gauge my mood, they would have been
wise enough to wait for the right opportunity. It seemed to

me that they were just concerned with what they wanted and not how it would affect me to give it to them. Perhaps that's what going on with you."

"Nah," Stuart says, "it can't be that simple!" He laughs.

I see him tracking with what I'm saying. "I'll bet you, if those guys in Hitch *spent a little more time understanding their subjects, they wouldn't have needed the services of Will Smith's character."*

For what it's worth, here is the rock bottom truth about all single people who are looking for a relationship: Everyone is nervous about being rejected and wonders if he or she will be accepted. Even the people who look the most confident and self-assured are just as clumsy and helpless as the rest of us. As you think about approaching someone, or how to respond to someone who is about to approach you, remember that you both have the rejection and acceptance issue in common. For the purpose of learning how to approach someone, it's imperative that you learn a little more about the core differences between men and women. So let's go to the Bible and read Genesis 2:18:

> *Then the LORD God said, "It is not good for the man to be alone. I will make a helper who is just right for him"* (NLT).

The Antidote to Aloneness

God created man, put him in the garden, and gave him action-oriented jobs to do—utilitarian, goal-oriented, functional, strap-on-the-tools and make-things-happen kind of work. But then God said it wasn't good for man to be alone. Notice that God didn't say anything about husbands and wives at this point. He just said something like, "I created the universe and humankind, but as good as it is, I don't like it that man is isolated and all alone." So God remedied the situation by giving man a companion to help him. God created woman—strange, wonderful, complex, beautiful woman.

Dr. Ronn

Help Meet

I'll share with you one of my most stupid blunders: Some Bible translations refer to man's companion as his "help meet." At the risk of making some women throw down this book, I'll admit I *used* to think of "meet" as M-E-A-T. Meat—meat that is going to help you, sustain you. Flesh created to help you be more alive and stronger. In my mind, woman was made to be something like an administrative assistant, somebody to take orders from the man. Are some of you men nodding your heads right now? You're probably thinking, *Well, isn't that correct? That's what I always believed!*

Pay attention, men, because I was wrong! That's not what the Word says, and that's certainly not what it means.

It's "help mate," as in M-A-T-E. The word "mate" comes from the word "measure" or "metric." It literally means help that measures up to a need. So what was the need? Did Adam need someone to shout orders to? Not at all! The need was actualized simply because man was alone. God said He wanted to solve the problem of aloneness, and He solved it by creating a female.

I stand corrected!

When God made woman, He created an antidote to human aloneness. Women are the *solution* to the problem of loneliness and isolation!

Sisters, you are the *remedy* that allows the possibility of intimacy. It means you were shaped, wired, created, designed, deployed, and positioned to solve what God says isn't good—aloneness.

At the very core, a woman's desires are in her DNA—blueprinted from Eve in the Garden of Eden. Woman has a relational purpose and function on this planet.

So a distinctly functional, utilitarian, goal-oriented Adam lived in the garden, and a relational Eve lived there with him. That doesn't mean Adam didn't know how to do relationship, and it doesn't mean Eve didn't know how to take care of business. It just means that, in God's creative design and intention, He wired men and women with both similarities and differences. And when you put those similarities and differences together, the possibility for an intimate love relationship, the possibility for partnership and exchange, and the possibility for balance is rich and full and glorious—and God calls that good.

But it's the *getting there* that feels foreign to us. Men are good at taking care of business in a relationship, but taking care of the business of initiating the relationship feels unnatural to many men. Women are good at nurturing and growing a relationship, but being the first to say hello or accepting a man's advances may make her feel like she's not built for relationships. The Bible doesn't say anything about Adam's or Eve's self-esteem at their first meeting, but then again, they didn't have to try and meet through an online dating service or on a blind date at a sushi bar. Clearly God took care of the issue of *getting there* for Adam and Eve. But us? Well, that's entirely a different matter.

Approach(able) 101

The basic principles of approaching someone involve understanding what motivates you to proceed and how the intended target of your affection is going to receive you.

The Man's Approach

Men, for example, show up and say, "I'm strapping on my tool belt, and I want to know (because I'm action-oriented) the places I can get the most return on my efforts."

================= *Walter says:* =================

I see her in church every Sunday, and we've made eye contact so I finally got up the nerve to talk to her. Compared to my usual half hour, I spent about two hours getting ready that morning. I looked good, I smelled good, and I knew what I was going to say. So I walked over and said, "I've been noticing you across the sanctuary, and I just wanted to come up and introduce myself to you."

She said, "My girlfriends are waiting for me outside. I'll have to check on you later." And that was that.

What happened? I showed up to get the job done, and there was no opportunity for me to succeed. The following week I saw her in church again, and she looked at me and smiled. So what do I do now?

I'm not ready to fly in for another approach if she's going to shoot me down again. I think I'll just wait to see if she comes over and talks to me. I don't know a lot about her, so I don't even know if she's worth the rejection I felt.

If a man feels the sting of rejection, he'll likely try again. Although he has been known to go back and try again with the same woman, he usually goes some other place. A man can only take so much rejection before he becomes a little more hesitant about approaching any woman that catches his eye. More men today are starting to wonder, *Why should I even try?* Thus, many women are looking around and trying to figure out where all the eligible and available men are!

> *The men who try to do something and fail are infinitely better than those who try to do nothing and succeed.*
>
> LLOYD JONES

The Thought Process of a Man. When it comes to relationships, the thought life of a typical man might look something like this: *Okay, this is what I'm going to do. I'm going to call her on the phone. And then I'm going to stop and pick up flowers. Then I'm going to take her to the movies. Then I'm going to surprise her and take her to a restaurant.*

Every time he accomplishes each thing on his list, he mentally crosses it off. *Okay, I'm done with that. Now when we're walking to the movie, I'm probably going to hold her hand. No, I'm going to wait until after the movie. Then I'll grab her hand, and we'll walk to the restaurant.*

He charts it out and crosses it off his list when he's done because a man approaches what he values most as something he needs to tend and care for. And that goes for approaching a woman too. Finding you, dating you, and loving you, ladies, are very important tasks to him—ones that he values and holds precious and sacred. But make no mistake, it's still a job to him.

So when he steps into church on Sunday morning, even before his hands come together in worship, he's looked around and checked things out. He's told himself, *Before the choir sings the second selection, I'm going to slide my way over here and see what's going on.*

Dr. Ronn

My Mental Checklists

When my wife, Aladrian, and I were dating long-distance, once each month we'd travel to see each other. We only had a limited window of opportunity for face-to-face inter-action so as I traveled by train, I'd pull out my pad and write down, "When I see her, I should probably hug her." *Okay,* I told myself, *I'm going to hug her.* Then I'd write, "I want to talk to her..." I wrote everything down, and then I'd mentally check each thing off as I did it. As I traveled back to LA, I would bask in the glory of how successful I was at completing everything on my list.

Oftentimes this mechanical behavior can be misinterpreted as a *defect,* but it's just the way God designed men. We are linear thinkers—once we've done something, we think it's finished. If we have to go back to it, we wonder why. "Okay, you're my girl. I have you. Why do I have to call you every day now? Let's move on to the next thing."

Even at the beginning of a relationship, men will think, *Let's see, she called me last week so I better call her this week. No, wait. I called her the last three times so I should e-mail her now.* He plots the course, then does it. The minute a man's eyes open in the morning, he's thinking, *What do I have to do today? And do I have what it takes to get it all done?*

This is exactly how a man's mind works when he approaches a woman for the first time—in a linear, plotted fashion that he's already rehearsed in his mind, even if it's just for a second. When a woman applauds this aspect of a man, she's packaging herself as a true blessing.

Receiving His Approach. A woman doesn't have to go to any extremes to accommodate a man's approach. As long as she doesn't humiliate him or make him feel as if his efforts are fruitless, she will be fine. It is helpful to understand that he's doing everything he can do to impress her.

Ladies, it's okay to say you're not available to *every*body or to *any*body, but you need to be available to explore the possibility of a relationship with a certain *some*body, And be willing to be uncomplicated about it. That means you can have a five-minute conversation without mentioning everything that was said in your therapy session yesterday or listing all of your generational curses. You don't have to report that you're on your thirtieth day of sobriety, and you certainly don't have to say, "Look here, I need to know right now if you're a dog or a decent guy because that last loser was a complete dog, and let me tell you what he did…"

When a man approaches, when he shows up to get the job done, it would be great to see more women open to his approach, to see uncomplicated women who are willing to say, "Yes, I'm available for this introduction to what might possibly turn into something more."

Jackie says:

Now that I look back at my dating relationship with Melvin, I remember signs that he was definitely an action-oriented tender and keeper type of guy. At first, I felt like I was dating some kind of robot! I had no idea what was going on in that man's head. I just kept thinking, this man does *not* know how to communicate! I had no idea he had more than one language to show his love for me. And I certainly didn't know he was all about actions and goals. That loud noise you hear? It's the sound of my hand slapping my forehead!

The Woman's Approach

One of the lame bills of goods sold to Christian women is that it's not ladylike for her to show interest in a man. But there is nothing wrong with a woman letting a man know about her availability by walking up to him and saying hello.

A man is not offended if you let him know you're interested and unafraid to talk to him. He will, however, be offended if you start off trying to dominate every moment of your time together.

In other words, there's nothing wrong with *you* approaching *him* and saying, "I noticed you last Thursday night at the church singles meeting, and you just seemed like an interesting person to have a five-minute conversation with. Are you available to talk?" You're not saying you want to run off and get married, or you want to be the mother of his three good-looking children, or you can't get to heaven without him. All you did was make it known that you're an uncomplicated, friendly person who might make a positive difference in his life without his feeling crushed by fear of rejection.

Alexandra says:

After last weekend I think I know how men feel when they get the snub from a woman. I was out with my girlfriends at the club, and this cute guy came up to Shelley and asked her to dance. Now this man looked nervous—as if he thought he was going to hell when Jesus comes back!

But even being nervous, he came over and asked her to dance. *Just* Shelley. He didn't make the mistake of asking her and when she said no, asking someone else at our table. We women just hate that. In fact, we don't usually let a guy like that get away without a few scratches!

Anyway, Shelley said, "No, I just want to sit here and talk with my girlfriends."

He was very polite about it, smiled, and went back to his friends. A few minutes later, I was on my way out the door when I saw him with one of his buddies. I heard him say, "If she just wants to sit and talk to her friends, why didn't they just stay home or sit in the car?"

Suddenly I understood how cruel we women must seem, so tempting and yet so unavailable. By the time I reached my car, I realized how often my girlfriends and I do that when we go out together. Sharing a dance doesn't mean we're committing to marriage!

So I did this crazy thing: I walked back and handed him my card and told him, "Call me next week and we'll go have coffee." I've never done that before, but this is one woman who isn't going to miss out on what might be a good opportunity!

I may catch a lot of flack for saying this, but women, by their very nature, should be very good at approaching men—perhaps even *better* than men. Now let's unpack this for a moment. Who is the one most likely to say, "We need to sit down and work out this issue"? Who is most likely to say, "I just e-mailed you an article, and I really think you should read it because it's talking about us"? Who says, "We need to set up a meeting to see the pastor and talk about this thing"? The man or the woman? Usually the woman. And it's because she is the antidote to human aloneness—the solution to true relationship and intimacy.

*Women wish to be loved without a why or a wherefore;
not because they are pretty, or good, or well-bred, or
graceful, or intelligent, but because they are themselves.*

HENRI FREDERIC AMIEL

Women don't generally look to be applauded for what they do. It's the sharing of nouns, verbs, adjectives, and emotions that spell out love to her. So when a woman steps out and makes the first move to introduce herself to a man, the question he should be asking is: What is utmost in her mind? Men, here's the guided tour answer to that mystery: It's the *reassurance* and *security* that there is the possibility of an intimate love relationship there, and included in that is the *sharing* of emotions, words, and experiences from each other's worlds. When she approaches, be ready to share. Clamming up or acting too cool for school shuts her down.

Dr. Ronn

A Mature Love

In chapter four I pointed out that you need to love another person the way God loves you—with forgiveness, grace, mercy, and selfless devotion. I explained the best way to receive the kind of love you want is to give to your partner the kind of love he or she needs.

Men, here is the bottom line: When you give away the kind of love you don't necessarily need for yourself, but you know it's the kind of love she needs—when you can be so unselfish as to graciously pour yourself into her and

> want nothing of that kind of love in return—then you've reached a mature milestone and you're on your way to successfully completing the task of loving her. And isn't that the ultimate goal?

The Thought Process of a Woman. Men are fairly complex creatures, but their complexities pale in comparison to the many faces of Eve. It might be easier to just count the stars. She has so many colors in her palette, so many moods and faces she must wear for the world. Most of us men either run scared or sit in awe at the female of our species. If we could just stand back and examine what she is up against every day and see things from her perspective, we'd have a much deeper appreciation for her approach. We'd also appreciate her long after the relationship begins.

You see, women have to be everything to all people. A woman looks at herself in the mirror and, like every man, she wonders if she has what it takes to get through this day. Even if the answer is a sheepish "maybe," she knows she still has to hit the ground running and not stop until she falls into bed at night.

In this series of sketches from some amazing women I've counseled, I'm going to show you just how many faces Eve might have to wear.

TRUDY ON
The Face I Wear for Coworkers and Colleagues

I realize I have to work smarter and faster because the competition is fierce. Even though women are holding more executive positions than at any other time in history, I feel like I'm still running twice as hard to get half as far as most men. But I can really shine in the workplace—even though there are times when it beats against my natural instincts to nurture and create harmony in relationships.

I can make the tough decisions in business, but always lingering in the back of my mind is the desire for harmony first. I'm always at odds with what my heart is telling me and what Wall Street demands.

BRENDA ON
The Face I Wear for My Parents

There comes a time in every woman's life when she looks at her parents and realizes they are aging. This struck me when the tables turned, and I was suddenly responsible for caring for them. It was a huge burden for me at first, but not in a negative sense. I just felt the need to lift this task and carry it through to completion. I want to do whatever is necessary to care for my mom and dad until the end of their lives.

SHARON ON
The Face I Wear for My Siblings

Sometimes I'm at odds with my brother and two sisters. At other times you can't tear us apart with a crowbar! And you better just stay out of it when it comes to my sisters. You'd be better off herding cats than trying to settle an issue between us!

Sometimes I have to be the strong one for my siblings, but there is an amazing submission process at work. It allows me to be very vulnerable with them and submit to their authority when necessary.

JACQUE ON

The Face I Wear for My Children

I usually have to do the approaching when it comes to dating because when a man finds out I have kids, he usually looks like he just remembered he left the gas on—and he's gone!

Seriously though, if a man wants to date me, he needs to be aware that during the dating process he will never be more important to me than my children are. He should never undermine my authority or show me disrespect in front of my kids because I would give my life for them or do whatever is necessary to protect them—with or without a man in my life.

JAMIE ON

The Face I Wear for My Friends

When I date a man, I try to make him understand the bond that exists between me and my girlfriends. Even though he's special to me, he can't fully understand or compete with my girls. Chick lit, chick flicks, girl's nights out, spa weekends, lengthy phone conversations, shopping, antique stores, flea markets—a man could get dizzy and fall down. He just needs to recognize that this is an important part of who I am and respect it from a distance.

A woman's heart is a deep ocean of secrets.

GLORIA STUART

Angie on
The Face I Wear for My Man

I want him to see all my many facets so he can know and love all of them. I'll pick up his shirts and remember all his family's birthdays, and I'll do it willingly because I love him and want to serve him flawlessly. But I need him to see me in every possible light—every flaw, every imperfection—and still tell me I'm beautiful to him.

I can be very flirtatious and coy in one breath and lay down the law in the next, and I want him to love both sides of me at once. You know, it really takes a lot to blow it with me, but if he does, he'll know it because I'll turn that face on him like the dark side of the moon. I think actor John Barrymore said it best, "The way to fight a woman is with your hat. Grab it and run."

Sarah on
The Face I Wear for My God

There is nothing more beautiful than a woman in prayer and worship! My prayer life with God is colorful and brilliant, but a man won't see that about me at first meeting. I have a secret life with God. He's the secret Lover of my soul. The man I fall in love with needs to know that there will be times when he can't be my hero. He won't be able to comfort me, and he can't be my everything. But he doesn't need to be jealous or insecure, because the one nearest and dearest to my heart is my Lord.

Dr. Ronn

The Face She Wears When She's Alone

Every woman, no matter how confident she appears, has a mark of vulnerability inside her. It may stem from a past hurt or rejection, a disappointment you know nothing of, a betrayal, a lie, or a broken promise. And every time she looks into a mirror, she sees that mark of vulnerability. She may have no idea how strong she can be, but she definitely knows how weak she can be. When she's alone and sees herself, she measures herself against other women who may appear (to her) to be sexier, thinner, smarter, and more successful. She constantly thinks of ways she can improve herself, her life, and the lives of those around her. Every woman places herself in some stage of training to be the perfect Proverbs 31 woman. Men will rarely, if ever, see this face of Eve. When and if you do, you know you've been invited into the inner chambers of her heart. It's a great honor to share that.

*Nothing makes a woman more beautiful
than the belief that she is beautiful.*

SOPHIA LOREN

Receiving Her Approach. If a man can see and appreciate all the faces of Eve, then he can recognize her subtle differences along with her vast complexities. Only then can men begin to appreciate what is going on behind the scenes when a woman approaches him and makes the first contact. All this information is valuable to a man long after the first hello, but having this knowledge beforehand definitely makes him a more approachable subject.

While the subject of a woman asking a man out on a date is still considered taboo in many circles, be confident that there is nothing wrong with a woman approaching a man and asking for five minutes of his time to have a conversation.

Men, a woman who approaches you isn't a desperate woman with loose morals. She's a confident woman who sees something in you that obviously fits into her plan. Like the way the fine point of a laser beam can find a target several miles away, a woman can spot her ideal match in a crowded room.

Men, too, have the option to say, "I'm flattered by your attention, but I'm not available." But if you are available and if you're trying to recognize your soul mate, it just might be that she's recognized you first!

Come On In, the Water's Fine

Here are some quick suggestions to help you prepare for a successful approach.

- Stop worrying about looking foolish. Chances are you'll be happier looking like a fool and getting rejected than kicking yourself later for not trying. Nothing ventured, nothing gained!

- When you approach, approach with confidence and a smile. Read the body language and keep the conversation moving.

- When approaching someone for the first time, try to start the conversation by asking questions relating to the current environment you're both in. That's an easy way to get the conversation started.

- Ask genuine questions that demonstrate how you've packaged yourself as a valuable asset to a relationship. Just remember, it's not a job interview or an application for life insurance!

- Remember to gauge the *real* reasons why someone would reject your approach. There are a million and one reasons why a person might say "no" one moment but "yes" the very next day. Sometimes the object of your approach is just having a bad day. Maybe he just doesn't feel like talking to anyone at that moment. Or maybe she's dating someone else or married. If that's the case, you don't really want her to accept your invitation anyway. You shouldn't take a "no" as a personal rejection of your wonderful self.

- Get some business cards that list your name and e-mail address. Nothing else—not a full description, not your measurements, not your job description or what kind of car you drive. Just those two things—name and e-mail address. You're not implying anything by giving it to someone. You're just offering them access to get to know you better, if they so desire. Giving someone your card makes you appear approachable.

- Don't forget this important part of your approach—closing the deal! That means you say hello, you have the initial conversation, give your contact info if it's appropriate, and you don't walk away without getting a phone number or an e-mail address from them. It doesn't do you a lot of good to get home, do your little victory dance, and then realize you have no way to contact him or her!

- Remember that it's okay for women to do the approaching. Distinguish yourself from your eight girlfriends who have locked arms on the way to the ladies' room. First look at him and make sure he sees you looking at him. Smile, walk over, and greet him warmly. You make yourself approachable that way. Approaching a man means you're taking responsibility for your love life, and there's nothing wrong with that.

- If someone approaches you and you're not interested, say so, but do it politely while looking that person in the eye. (You might prepare a graceful rejection line, so that you're not caught with an awkward pause or—worse—a white lie such as "Uh, I was just leaving.") Show respect for the person who had the guts to approach you, but don't feel obligated to say "yes" when you really mean "no." It's not about saving someone from hurt feelings. That would be a relationship built on dishonesty.

- On that note, if someone tells you he or she isn't interested, then don't pry to see if he or she really means it. If you doubt the "no" was permanent, then try again another time. But know when to walk away. You don't want to pester someone into going out with you. Remember, there are stalking laws!

- One last thing for the record: Approaching does *not* mean you are desperate!

You're on the downhill slope now! This chapter has been all about approaching someone you're interested in spending more time with and how to make yourself more approachable, so you don't miss out on those potentially fantastic opportunities for relationships.

What happens now that you know what you want in a mate, how you present yourself to a prospective partner, where the best match for you can be found, and how you walk up to that person and say hello or receive his or her invitation to have a conversation? Eventually (and I'm betting it will be soon) you're going to have to go on that date.

What's Next?

After you figure out where you'll go on your date, after you mull over what you'll wear, and after you arrive and look at each other across a table, you'll have to start revealing things about yourself. How much do you reveal? How deep should it get? What do you say? What don't you say?

In chapter eight you'll learn the process of exposing the real you. You'll figure out what kind of personality you have in relationships and when to release just the right amount of information so that a strong relationship progresses at appropriate intervals.

What's Behind Your Fig Leaf?

We all have them. We all hide behind them. We're all ashamed and anxious about being unloved because of them. Don't even try to deny it—you have fears.

Perhaps it's that the end of your life will come and you will have always felt misunderstood, unloved...unlovable. Maybe it's something else. But it's a question you must answer: What's behind *your* fig leaf? What do you fear?

Think about the relationships that started out great—the first week was amazing, the first month was incredible, the first six months went...fairly well...but some time between the storybook beginning and the horror movie ending, something happened. You thought, *This is just another person who can't accept me for who I really am.*

But maybe that person never got to see who you really are. Maybe all they saw was the initial good impression, and then they saw your fig leaves. Your "love substitutes."

Love substitutes are the things you hide behind to keep from being open with another person. There are many love substitutes—more than we look at in this book. But there are some typical ones that I've discovered generally fit most of the people I counsel about relationships.

As you read about these typical love substitutes, you may hit on one and think, *Oh, that's definitely me!* But you're more likely to see yourself scattered between two or three. That's normal.

When it happens, I want you to ask God to help you identify your love substitutes and take the actions I prescribe for each one.

You may find this a difficult chapter, so please take a moment and meditate on this prayer that will help you open up to deeper places in your heart.

May God bless you as you undertake this difficult step. May He open your heart to the truth behind your fear and reveal to you the things you've been using as substitutes for the pure and perfect love He put inside you. I pray that all the pretense, all the denial, all the pride that come with your fig leaves will be wiped away to reveal a new body, a new mind, and a new heart in Christ—ready to be shared with another person. Let the psalmist's words ring true in your ears: "The Lord is on my side; I will not fear. What can man do to me?" (Psalm 118:6 NKJV). Amen.

If you find it too difficult to handle this step on your own, please seek the counsel of trusted family members or your most honest friends. Your pastor can help you work through these issues too.

Starting now, you are going to be a person who understands what you fear, and you're going to begin conquering that fear. You have a God who is strong enough to take your fear and carry it. After all, He has promised He would never leave you or forsake you, and that means *never.*

8

Reveal Yourself—And Be Real

Do not be afraid, for I have ransomed you. I have called
you by name; you are mine.

ISAIAH 43:1 NLT

✄

I've never counseled anyone as self-centered as Byron. I can
openly write this because Byron freely admits it.

"Yes, most of the time it really is all about me," Byron
says. "As soon as Linda realizes that I am the man in this
relationship and that I do know what is best, then we can
stop playing these little games of hers and get down to the
business of planning a wedding."

I can't even speak for a second because I'm absolutely
dumbfounded.

"You're a man," he says, "so surely you agree with my
assessment." It wasn't a question. He was telling me that I
agree with him. Hmm. Lord, give me patience.

"Byron, why does anything have to be about you?" He
looks at me like he's just swallowed a bug.

"You obviously don't understand," Byron sputters, "so I'll
just spell it out for you. I bring home the bacon, and it's a lot.
I'm paying for everything. I have more years of experience in
the real world. My friends and business associates have been
cultivated over a long period of time, and those relationships
are very influential and lucrative for my future. I want our
wedding to be a small and exclusive affair, and we just
don't have room on our guest list for some of Linda's...well,
less-cultured family members and friends. I offered to let her

have a little party when we come back from the honeymoon
so she could invite all those kinds of people she knows."

"Byron, let me ask you something." I begin what will be
a long journey with him—and I know it may not end at
the wedding altar. "What are you afraid of?"

I know it's never a good thing to have someone tell you that you're going to fail, that it's inevitable, and there's nothing you can do about it. It makes you think, *Why should I even try?* But the truth is that failure is part of all relationships. Sometimes when you lose, you win. It's all in how you handle a fall.

Your Fear Introduced

Adam and Eve fell. They fell hard. And when they fell, something happened in the garden that has followed us through history and into the present day. Let me take you there to see what happened. In Genesis 3:8-9 (NLT) it says:

> *When the cool evening breezes were blowing,*
> *the man and his wife heard the LORD God walking about in*
> *the garden. So they hid from the LORD God among the trees.*
> *Then the LORD God called to the man,*
> *"Where are you?"*

The next verse, verse 10, is revealing because Adam responds to God by saying, "I heard you walking in the garden, so I hid. I was afraid" (NLT). He was afraid! One minute we have a perfect love relationship with God and with each other, and the next minute we're hiding and afraid. Suddenly a new emotion is introduced into our love relationship with each other!

But why was Adam afraid? He was afraid because he was naked, so he hid from God behind a couple of little fig leaves. But wait a minute—he was naked earlier and wasn't afraid, so what happened?

First of all, the word *naked* doesn't historically mean "undressed."

In Mandaic-Aramaic, naked also means "void" and "empty." Adam is afraid he is defective and dysfunctional, and his fig leaves are substitutes for the confidence he should have in God and in God living in him.

Imagine what happened when God questioned Adam, "What's the matter with you, man? First you run from Me, as if you could actually *hide* from Me, and now you're talking like a crazy person. Who told you that you're naked?"

And man—big, strong, utilitarian, Built Ford Tough man—says, "Well, You remember that woman You gave me? You know, the one I didn't ask for? I went to sleep, woke up and felt this little pain in my side, and when I looked up, this *girl thing* You put there just started talking. And she told me about this fruit. Well, let me tell you what happened next. You know that serpent? I *know* I didn't ask for serpents, but down came this serpent, and it told me about the fruit too…so I ate it."

Fear and blame! Flimsy little fig leaves. But the world is choked with the abundance of them. Everybody is looking for a new way to cover what is "naked" about themselves.

Your Shame Revealed

It began in the garden and continues today. The fig leaves of fear and blame temporarily cover up what is imperfect about us, and for the past couple of centuries, we've perfected this little practice to an art form.

Christian psychologist and best-selling author Larry Crabb wrote a book called *The Silence of Adam,* and he hit this topic right between the eyes.

> What if life exposes me as a failure, someone who cannot handle its legitimate demands? What if I am unable to deal effectively with matters that I must admit are truly important? What if I ruin everything—my family, my friendships, my job—and I am left alone, a loser standing naked for everyone to see? What if I face the fact that

all my money, possessions, and good times haven't filled
that awful emptiness deep inside?[11]

This is the true source of fear. It's based in shame, and that shame
erupted when we broke covenant with God for the first time. It's
been sort of our curse ever since. We feel shame about not being
good enough, and that shame evokes fear—fear that we'll be found
out as the imposters we are—and that fear manifests itself in the
most vulnerable place: our relationships with each other and with
God.

We are all wired to want at least one other person on this planet
to know and love us, in spite of and in light of everything that person
knows about us. We want somebody to see all the junk. We want
somebody to admire and applaud our pearly white teeth, all shining
and glowing—even when they're in a glass on the bedside table.

So now we're at cross-purposes. We really want the kind of love
God wants for us with the wonderful person God has planned for
us, the person we don't have to hide all our junk from. But we're too
afraid of failure and too afraid of being hurt. We're too afraid to show
another person everything inside us because if they knew *everything,*
then they would know exactly where to stick the knife and exactly
when to twist it.

So we dress up our fears to hide them. When we're hurt by enough
people and we've failed enough times, we become quite sophisticated
about the ways we cover up our fears.

If you're planning to enter into a long-term love relationship with
someone, you can't ignore your fears or your fig leaves anymore. Sooner
or later you have to dig down to the roots of your fears and face them.
Making this choice involves a series of steps, which revolve around the
frightening idea that, yes, we want to pursue an outcome that, no, we
cannot guarantee.

The first step is facing the fears and replacing love substitutes with
the real deal.

"There is no fear in love. But perfect love drives out fear." That's what First John (NIV) 4:18 says. And that describes God's love for me. It took me a long time to realize God's love is a perfect love, and it's the *only* perfect love available.

Yeah, there was a time when I acted like I had no fear. But I was so afraid of hurt and rejection, and I was blanketing those fears with so much strategy and game that I didn't even recognize myself anymore. I knew the only way I could successfully navigate dating and waiting for *the one* was to ruthlessly and boldly face my fears with the knowledge that God's perfect love surrounds me. Until I got to that point, I was very lonely all the time and made a lot of bad choices about my relationships.

Ultimately I had to choose between safety and security in my own mistakes. I had to walk out onto that limb and say, *Lord, I take steps away from the security of self-sabotaging love substitutes, and I take baby steps toward what scares the heck out of me—the ability to love somebody Your way, even when I don't have all the guarantees of where this is heading.*

Your Fig Leaf Defined

I mentioned at the beginning of this section that there are many names for how we cover our fear, and that those names take different forms on men and women. It's time to define the most predominant fig leaves and determine which ones you wear.

If you're sitting there and thinking, *Well, I know I won't fit into any of them. I just don't have those problems.* Stop! We all fall, remember? Even the best of us. So check that pretense at the door and let's get started.

The Dreamer
Fear: Loss of the Perfect Opportunity

One thing is true for everyone at the beginning of relationships: The excitement and newness distract attention away from things that may challenge the relationship later.

Everyone has flaws that can bring friction into a relationship, but passion can make the flaws seem insignificant. The problems become harder to ignore as the relationship begins to need more than just passion to make it grow and still maintain all the hopeful joy.

Dr. Ronn

The Dreamer

There is an old story about a village whose corn crop had failed, so there was no seed for the coming planting season. A young woman from that village decided to travel to a distant village for help. When she arrived, the woman approached the town elder and explained her village's need. The elder took the woman to his village's corn field and told her she could choose seed from any single ear of corn in one particular row. It was a very long row of corn. The chief told her, "You can walk down this row, examine the ears of corn as you walk, but you may not choose the ears you have already passed."

The woman eventually came to the end of the row...and

never chose. As she walked, she kept hoping to find a larger ear of corn on the next stalk. Thus the women went home to her village empty-handed.

That's the story of the Dreamer's life—always waiting for something better to come along, never choosing, always losing out.

Case Study: Brett

Brett is a fine Christian man with loads of charisma, but he's hiding behind the typical Dreamer fig leaf.

In the beginning of new relationships, Brett is a hero—the true blue champion. He is always the first in the relationship to start making hopeful plans for the future. He makes promises, honestly believing he will prove faithful where others before him have fallen short. He's even involved his family in new relationships on many early occasions, making the woman he was dating feel like part of his family.

But here is where Brett gets into trouble. He freely enters relationships and enjoys the blind ecstasy of the early stages, but then he quickly cools when things aren't easy anymore—or worse, when he finds someone else who provides newer joy and a fresher fantasy.

Brett swears he's not a "player" who intends to have multiple relationships. He vows he doesn't have a problem with commitment. He just quickly develops the urge to break things off when doubt or disappointment sets in. As this occurs, he has little awareness of his pattern of deception. Brett has even gone so far as to use God in his deceit. He's actually told women, "I'm sorry. God just didn't choose you for me after all."

So why does Brett do it? Because he's driven by the fear of missing out on a better thing. He believes no relationship is good enough to commit to and develop, and he refuses to settle for anything less than what he imagines is the "perfect mate" and the "perfect relationship."

There is no doubt that Brett lives in a fantasy world of perfect circumstances that don't exist in the real world. The perfection will never come, of course, and he'll continue to move from one short-lived relationship to the next. As time goes on, he'll become weaker and less ready to serve in a real other-centered relationship.

Character strength gets you through the rough spots that bring growth in relationships. But Brett's fear has replaced his character strength. To put it bluntly, Brett is selfish.

True partnership involves walking with someone when they don't look their best, not just when things are exciting and delightful. True partners learn how to stick together through the little betrayals that naturally happen in relationships because they know people in relationships will, at some point, disappoint each other. But they get past the hurt in a way that actually *grows* the relationship.

Brett, however, lets the slightest disappointment ignite his fear factor, and he then ends the relationship. Unfortunately, the heaviest cost to Brett has been a cycle of recurring loss, dissatisfaction, and periods of intense loneliness.

How does Brett get out from under his fig leaf? First, Brett has to go back to the beginning where he first believed the lie that put him on the fantasy path of deception and perfectionism. He must reject the lie that there is a perfect mate and a perfect relationship, and that he will somehow lose something if he commits to a relationship that isn't like Christmas every day.

Brett must learn that there are many exhilarating mountaintop experiences to be had on a regular basis in a relationship, and he should expect and appreciate them when they come. But he has to know that in between those mountaintop experiences are a lot of ordinary times, challenges, and even some painful moments that, when combined, build a truly satisfying relationship.

Imperfections aren't bad! If life was perfect and if people were perfect, we wouldn't need each other—and we wouldn't need God. In God's eyes, being perfect means we are complete in Him. In God's eyes, the perfect relationship is one in which two people are complete before they get together—they can then complete each other when they become a couple. They are safe with each other in the midst of their flaws.

Even Jesus didn't want "perfect" disciples to share His love. He was committed to them when they listened, when they followed Him, *and* when they were a pain in the neck. Jesus chose broken, flawed, willful people to become His voice in the world—people who would learn to trust His strength, instead of fig leaves, to cover their fears and imperfections.

===== *Leon says:* =====

Dr. Ronn, let me read an e-mail I got from Belinda—an *e-mail* and not the courtesy of a face-to-face conversation: "I appreciate all that God has done in our relationship during the last year. I learned so much from you and I believe that you're a really wonderful person who will have no trouble establishing the kind of relationship you deserve. However, the Lord has spoken to me and revealed that this is not my season. The Lord has someone else in mind for me."

Wow! I thought we were reaching milestones in our relationship, going through some tough times, growing in our struggles together...I guess not.

Are you a Dreamer? If you recognize yourself in this case study, I want to encourage you to start over and develop a new vision of what a real relationship is. It isn't about *settling for less* from a relationship—it's about *investing more* into a relationship. A true relationship isn't a place where someone meets your expectations and fills your emptiness. It's a place where your love makes it safe for an imperfect person to be with you.

Perhaps you should even consider refraining from starting a new relationship and spend some time in counseling with your pastor or a group of friends who won't cut you any slack. Bring your family members in if they've seen you in action. But while you're going through this period of discovery, while you're lifting the fig leaf to see the ugly truth that lies beneath it, don't start a new relationship.

When the time comes for you to start dating again (or if you're already in a relationship), watch for those yellow flags that sent you running in the past. Stand strong and ride those times out. Talk through those times with your pastor or friends. Listen to what they're telling you because they'll know you better than you know yourself.

Most of all, embrace the chaos and use the tough times as times for growth—personally and in your love relationships.

Dr. Ronn

The Illusion of Hypocrisy

The most self-centered people I counsel say things such as, "Wouldn't I be a complete hypocrite if I did something that was the opposite of my instincts and I didn't feel it?"

This is what I tell them. "You have put your emotions on a throne as if they are bigger than anything else in your life. It's time to check those emotions at the door and act by *faith* instead! If your fears tell you to run your mouth, shut up for a while. The price you'll pay for doing the opposite is merely tolerating the stress for a short time. Just fake it until you make it! And let your emotions catch up later. You do the opposite because the old way is dead to you. It's a dead horse, and you have to leave it and move on."

"But wait," some will continue to argue, "that horse may be dead, but it's a familiar dead horse. I'm used to that dead horse. And I know it's ugly and smelly, but it's my dead, ugly, smelly horse!"

You can argue until Jesus comes back, but my message will never change. "That horse is dead, never to be revived. Leave it where it lies and move on."

The Controller
Fear: Failure and Making Mistakes

Controllers are similar to Dreamers because they tend to be perfectionists. They also fear that their failure will expose their inadequacies and weaknesses. Controllers aren't just afraid of failure in relationships, but in all they do and all that others say about them.

Case Study: Kate

Kate is convinced that if she makes a mistake or allows someone she cares about to make a mistake, it will cast doubt on her personal worth, and she will somehow be responsible for the negative results.

People close to Kate believe she has a huge ego, but the truth is that her self-esteem is actually quite fragile. She has to be right all the time, and when it's obvious (even to her) that she is wrong, she reinterprets her error in a way that preserves her right to impose her leadership upon others.

In the beginning of new relationships, Kate wants to know everything about her man, but she's very guarded and uncomfortable about revealing anything sensitive about herself. Such transparency would mean letting go of too much control. Even Kate's closest friends say it's a supreme compliment for her to open up meaningfully because of the deep trust it would require from her.

So why does Kate do it? Kate believes she can only trust herself to protect what's valuable to her. Her fear of failing to protect herself and those she cares for from the consequences of mistakes is about one thing: control.

Dr. Ronn

The Controller

Men and women are a little different in how they behave as Controllers. A male Controller is more heavy-handed and will even impose his will by force. At that point it is probably more a matter of preserving his dignity as a man than fulfilling his duties as a leader or protecting others.

A female Controller is usually a little more subtle and manipulative in maintaining control. Her objective is to convince others that it is in their best interest to comply with her wishes, even if it's just to end the conflict.

Kate has no idea of the crushing effect her pressured leadership has on others. Her relationships weaken and often die because only she is allowed to have free will. Only she is allowed to make mistakes and learn from them. Only she knows what is best for everyone. People who are close to Kate, or who begin to get close to her, will learn their hearts are not safe with her.

Her close friends, her boyfriends, her future husband, even her children will begin to feel like nonpersons and eventually withdraw. In the worst case scenario, Kate's children will grow up emotionally guarded and insecure, which may result in their developing controlling patterns of their own.

How does Kate get out from under her fig leaf? First and foremost, she has to confess this sin to God, repent of it, and begin learning the most important lesson her life: to put her whole trust in God's strength. It will help Kate to compare her ways to the example of Jesus.

Even though He was God in the flesh, Jesus still lived as a man who was totally abandoned to the strength of the Father. Like Jesus, Kate must abandon her strength. However, unlike Kate, Jesus was the perfect leader. He didn't fall for the devil's temptations, and He didn't make mistakes. Kate must embrace the knowledge that mistakes will occur, not all decisions will be the best ones, and people aren't perfect—she isn't perfect and no amount of control will ever make it so.

Are you a Controller? You do have certain responsibilities that require appropriate levels of control. But your first responsibility is to have self-control over your fear and your urge to impose inappropriate control over things and people. You must grow your trust in God's lordship over your life and the lives of everyone you are feverishly trying to protect.

However, be aware that in your addiction to control, you may even try to take control of your spiritual growth. You may impose unrealistic standards of progress and then enforce a pressured, unbalanced life on yourself in order to satisfy those standards. If you do this, you'll inevitably do the same to others.

Remind yourself daily that God is responsible for your discipleship. Your job is to walk lovingly in the light you gain from a balanced Christian life and expect that God will continually give you more. One of the benefits of humbling yourself in this way will be the life-giving effect it will have on your love relationships.

Dr. Ronn

Moving from Fear Strategy to Love Strategy

I have a definition for my fear strategy: It is first and foremost what benefits *me*. In other words, I don't care what my fears do to you as long as my number one need is met—looking out for my fear. And if I have to choose between these two things: looking out for you and looking out for me, guess which one I'll pick? Sadly, that's what fear does to you. It makes you a very selfish and self-centered person.

The opposite of your fear strategy is a love strategy. A love strategy proclaims: In the way I have used fear to avoid, control, please, satisfy, or serve myself, I will now do the opposite.

The Avoider
Fear: Rejection

Avoiders have been severely emotionally injured by rejection at some point in their lives. As adults, Avoiders fear the pain and the impact any kind of rejection has on their self-esteem.

Case Study: Raji

Raji lives by the logic that he won't suffer abandonment, heartbreak, or rejection if he only has good friends and no romantic attachments. To avoid rejection in relationships, he has learned the art of making very good friends and being very clever at making sure his relationships never mature into romances.

He is a great encourager of romance for his friends and even plays matchmaker on occasion. In fact, matchmaking is one of the ways he can redirect romantic advances from others! When a woman shows an interest in him or crosses his comfort zone, he simply and politely dismisses the advance, and mentions the idea of introducing the woman to one of his wonderful and eligible friends.

Raji says he secretly wants a romantic relationship, but his fear drives him into avoidance mode.

Dr. Ronn

The Avoider

Avoiders engage in a kind of relationship karate. They instantly react to any perceived romantic threat with a collection of defense maneuvers that are designed to block or redirect it. If that fails, Avoiders will run or employ more verbally lethal strikes to end the advance.

So why does Raji do it? There are libraries full of textbooks containing reasons why people fear rejection. For some, it may have started in childhood with the rejection of a parent. For others, and this is Raji's case, they suffer a terrible heartbreak. When Raji was a young man, a girl broke his heart in a cruel way. He simply never recovered. He never dealt with the rejection. Therefore, he goes through life bearing the burden of feeling unlovable. The pain keeps him from trusting anyone with his heart, so he puts on a smile and pretends that love is for everyone except him.

How does Raji get out from under his fig leaf? Most people learn lessons in one place—the school of hard knocks. Just because Raji went to school and got knocked once doesn't mean he's finished. He's going to have to step out in faith and be willing to take a few more knocks before settling down to a life with the woman who will call his heart home.

The next time a woman shows an interest in Raji, he's going to need a *love strategy* to replace his *fear strategy,* and that means he has to do the opposite of what he would normally do. His first inclination is to divert the pass, but instead he needs to receive it and run for the goal line.

Even better, Raji needs to pay attention to his masculine intuition when he's attracted to a woman and actually approach her rather than wait for her to approach him. When he can do that, he'll really know he's on the road to a successful love relationship.

Are you an Avoider? Worse yet, are you that special kind of "Christian" Avoider who works this scheme because you can blame your unavailability on "God's current direction in your life" or a "spiritual journey you must travel alone"?

These can be honest statements for any Christian, but examine your heart on this one. Are you just using this as an awful excuse not to be involved with someone? If you are, it's dishonest and, worse, an abuse of your relationship with God.

You must know that the cost of being an Avoider is the loss of true intimacy and probably a pretty stifled life. When you build fences to guard yourself from possible pain, you forbid most other possibilities as well! It is through the positive and negative experiences in growing and unpredictable relationships that many of the most powerful changes in your life can take place.

I challenge you to risk being honest with God. I challenge you to face your fear of relationship pain and rejection and trust God with the direction of your relationships. God has a plan for you but you must look for it. In order to find the life God has for you, you must seek it out, knock on God's door, and ask for it. You must pursue life with a good conscience. Be wise and faithful to God and don't let your fears cripple your ability to make new connections and consider new love relationships.

The Pleaser
Fear: Rejection and Abandonment

Pleasers are similar to Avoiders because they fear rejection and abandonment. The fig leaf they hide behind is the way they devote themselves to keeping their partners happy so there will be no reason to be rejected.

Case Study: Judy

Judy is a master at developing alter egos. She will go out of her way to become the woman her man expects her to be. She has developed a keen ability to size up a person's desires and then put on a disguise that looks like the woman he wants.

In her current relationship, she loves jazz and smoky bars because her boyfriend loves jazz and smoky bars—even though her last boyfriend hated jazz and smoky bars (and, therefore, Judy hated jazz and smoky bars). The real question is: Does Judy really like jazz? Who knows?

Judy is putting on a continual puppet show and pulling her own strings according to whatever she thinks will win his applause. But the applause she seeks isn't the kind most of us enjoy hearing in response to doing good work. Judy feels rewarded when she believes she'll temporarily ward off rejection of who she *really* is.

Dr. Ronn

The Pleaser

One very tragic reality of the female Pleaser is that she will often find herself in an abusive relationship. Because she doesn't assert her true self, she doesn't have any real boundaries. No man can respect her.

In the abusive relationship, she covers up her codependency by claiming she has to give God time to work on her abuser. But she's not letting God work on the abuser—she's just using faith talk to cover up the true motives of *her* behavior. She's busy taking full responsibility for managing the direction of the relationship and adapting her behavior and personality to try to manipulate her abuser's behavior.

She feels powerless to live free of her tragic lifestyle because she doesn't believe she can be accepted any other way. She hangs on to that familiar place of control, even if it's in an abusive relationship.

So why does Judy do it? Judy is an imposter. She's afraid that if a man finds out who she really is, what she really likes and dislikes, he will reject her and she will be alone. Even though Judy feels stronger by being a Pleaser, she really has no control at all.

Ultimately, the price Judy pays is that she loses herself, and no one ever gets to know who she really is. Even if she entered into a normal, healthy-looking relationship, she wouldn't be able to grow because she's already lost her identity. Sadly, because she is constantly trying to avoid conflict and rejection, there is little potential for growth in her love relationships too.

How does Judy get out from under her fig leaf? In my opinion, this fig leaf is the one that requires the most professional help because most Pleasers are either in abusive relationships right now, or have been in abusive relationships in the past. If there hasn't been any abuse, there likely will be if the Pleaser does not receive intervention and counseling.

Being a Pleaser is a strong codependency issue, so Judy must first spend time with her pastor or a professional counselor to help her understand what triggers her choices and deal with them head-on. There are a number of fantastic books that deal with codependency issues—especially the books in the *Boundaries* series by Dr. Henry Cloud and Dr. John Townsend.[12] Judy should study these books and find a professional group of women that is dealing with these issues. She is definitely going to need some support and accountability.

Are you a Pleaser? You must know you won't enjoy the freedom of a Christ-centered life and a Christ-centered relationship until your fear of rejection is no longer at the center of your fear strategy. You must lay down your false identities and learn to accept who God is helping you to become, whether or not anyone else accepts you.

Look honestly at your past agenda for what it is—emotional suicide. Your weapon is a pack of lies about who you are. You've become addicted to your codependent relating style.

God will continue to deal with your addiction, sometimes harshly, until you hate it enough to abandon it and rely on Him to set you free. Remember, God does His best work in you through the challenges you overcome by trusting Him. He can't do much with the things you hide except to turn up the heat on them until you can't hide them anymore.

Be the person God envisions, not the person you think you must be to prevent rejection. This will require you to be willing to expose the truth about yourself and your life in general. Situations, of course, will determine how much you tell, but trusting God with your life means you no longer have to distort the truth about yourself to cover what you believe is unacceptable.

Make no mistake! Your faith will be challenged! Having boundaries means they will be tested. Telling the truth will sometimes alter the directions of even casual relationships. But in the long run, good healthy relationships will always be strengthened when the goal is to please God first.

The Real You Exposed

Now you've prayerfully considered any fig leaves you might have been hiding behind. You've decided to deal with them by using a love strategy, not a fear strategy. You've taken a good long look at the real you, and you're ready to unveil that person. The time will most definitely arrive when you have to do one of two things:

1. Reveal more about yourself than you've felt comfortable revealing in the past. *Do you know him?* The man who seems to look good on the outside, but it's easier to nail Jell-O to a tree than to have a conversation with him. He clams up, or he can't seem to focus because he's so nervous and so busy trying to bury you with his game.

2. Reveal less information than you're used to revealing. *Do you know her?* She's the woman who wants to tell you her entire life story in the first twenty minutes of meeting her, and afterward you feel like you just need a nap or a good cry.

Revealing More

Revealing the real you is more than just conquering your fears. Your first exposure to potential partners is when they get their first snapshot of you. It's the time when you get to release your "promotional package." Promotions are planned and handled with great care, so knowing *what* to release and *when* to release it is important to building trust and integrity into a relationship. Here are some of the best tips on how to expose the real you for the best possible success.

Your Signature Style. At least one person has told you how great you look in a certain color or a certain style of clothes. You may have a real flair for decorating your house or throwing parties. You might have a way you style your hair or apply makeup that is so dramatic that people stop you on the street to admire your work. These types of things create your style.

Some folks have a natural ability for putting colors and patterns together, while others are more like a fish on a bicycle when they have to pick out socks to match a tie. If you need help creating your personal style, pick up any popular fashion magazine and flip through the pages to find all sorts of ideas that look great—most of the time you can accomplish the look inexpensively. If you need more help in this area, go to the library or search the Internet for ideas. Most women would probably like to get together with some of their friends and talk about a signature style they want to put together for themselves. Men are more likely to quietly observe other men they admire, either in person or in the media, and make mental notes of clothing styles or other physical attributes.

Read books! Lots of books. Read books on decorating and how to throw great parties. Read books on fashion and makeup, furniture, art, bodybuilding, or any other topic that will help you create a definitive style people will remember.

Your signature style will be one of the first things people notice about you, and it will be a lingering memory as well.

Your Core Values and Beliefs in Action. You usually have to spend more than five minutes with someone to find out what they value and what they believe in. And because it's fairly deep conversational material, it is probably best to wait until a date or two have passed before you have the all-inclusive conversation about core values.

However, sometimes it is very easy to identify one or two core values when you first meet a person. Ladies, if you meet a man who starts talking about sex within the first five minutes, then you can guess that his values (and his respect for you) are faltering. Men, if you meet a woman for the first time and she immediately wants to know what was on your tax return last year, then you can estimate what she values most.

There are ways to superficially convey what you value at first meetings without seeming to be a superficial person. If you talk warmly about your parents, it's clear that you place a high value on family. If you are kind to service staff at a restaurant or in a store, it's evident that you value civility. If you help someone cross the street, open the door for someone, or give up your seat for an elderly person, it's clear that you value kindness and respect. You shouldn't do these things just because you're trying to impress someone. You should do them all the time no matter who is looking.

On the other hand, if these actions come naturally to you and they are part of your everyday behavior, you shouldn't *not* do them because you think you'll be portraying too nice of an image. There is no such thing as bargain basement values. You either have them or you don't. And if you have them, show them.

Your Subtle Spirituality. No one will know at first glance how spiritual you are. It's only after they meet and talk to you that they see that your integrity comes from God.

You don't have to walk into a room with your hands up in the air and praising God. And you don't have to hide your light under a bushel. Just be your kind, generous, compassionate, respectful, loving self at all times, even when no one is looking. Let your spirituality come out naturally as you meet and spend time with people.

A person who truly loves the Lord and follows His commands is easily recognized as an approachable person. When you meet someone and start having that five-minute conversation, your tone and the words you choose will reflect God's image—you shouldn't even have to tell them you are a Christian. Let the Holy Spirit be your consultant in this area.

Your Emotional Maturity. We tend to wear our emotions on our faces and in our body language, so it's easy to convey our emotional mix at first meetings. In other words, emotions don't lie, and anyone who sees you and talks to you for a few minutes will be able to know if you're tense, stressed, angry, depressed, or tired. They'll also be able to tell if you're a person with strong, positive emotions like happiness and joy.

It goes without saying that you should avoid any initial conversations that evoke powerful emotional responses from either of you.

An honest emotional response mixed with the nervousness of a first meeting could give an inaccurate reading of what your true emotional maturity is. Keep it light, keep it simple. It's okay to let another person know you have emotions and that you're not a dead fish. Just don't start crying when you hear the music from the diamond commercial and start pouring out the sad tale of your last failed marriage or engagement. There is a time to share your brokenness. The first meeting is not that time.

Dr. Ronn

Exposing Yourself

Exposing yourself in a relationship is a lot like getting to the center of an artichoke. The outer layers are harder in substance and more difficult to penetrate. But as you work at it and get closer to the center, you find it is soft and tender. The center is where the good stuff is, and the center is where you and a potential mate will want to go.

Mysteries Unsolved (and We Like It That Way!)

We've established that you will have to open yourself up to closer investigation sooner or later. But remember, it's still in your control because you get to choose who gets inside for a closer look. Again, you have to decide what and how much a person will see.

Slowly unraveling your mysteries to a potential mate should be done by unlocking a series of channels. That's right. Some things should have an element of mystery to them. For instance, everybody loves to keep their secret recipes secret (that's why they're called *secret* recipes). When he tastes your apple pie, his eyes roll back. When she has one sip of your coffee, she wants to know what you did to make it taste so good. Those little mysteries are what people remember about you—and it's what makes people want to know more.

Upon first meeting someone, if you share every little bit of information, every secret, every dream, every desire, and every disappointment, you leave nothing to the imagination and nothing for the future. There are a few definitions for the word "coy," but a degree of it makes first meetings a wonderful experience.

Here's a simple rule of thumb for you: Treat your good stuff like money—keep a little, save a little, give a little away. But do enjoy the mystery and let it linger as long as possible.

Sylvia says:

I have a couple of good girlfriends who know all my tricks! We actually learned about our love substitutes together so we agreed to spill the beans. Since then we've really worked hard for each other.

I've tried monitoring myself in relationships, but I'm only fooling myself. I know I have a Controller personality and that looks like wisdom to me. At least I'm wise enough now to know I can't hide behind that old fig leaf anymore. It's been my security blanket, my mask.

My girlfriends keep me in check. They know how I dress up my flaws to make them look like virtues, and they remind me that love is *other*-centered, and it's not about me. They know when I'm acting out of fear instead of love, and they'll say, "There you go, Sylvia, acting like your old self again!"

Now don't get me wrong. My friends aren't perfect! We're

just crazy in different areas so we help each other. We cover each other's blind spots, if you know what I'm saying.

It Works!

There are some simple rules to engaging in a conversation with a potential mate that will help expose more about him or her, and help you share your true self. Here are some tips to get you started:

- When you don't know what to say, ask a question. Asking questions is a great way to start or keep a conversation going. Most people like to talk about themselves. But be careful not to *only* ask questions, otherwise it starts to sound more like an interview than a conversation. Here are some great conversation-starter questions:

  » What do you like to do?

  » Do you have any pets?

  » Have you ever _____?

  » What places have you traveled to?

  » What's your favorite book, movie, or sports team?

  » What's your favorite restaurant or kind of food?

  » Where did you go to school?

- If you often find yourself in situations where you don't know what to say, then do some homework and find some topics you can have a conversation about.
- Practice talking about new topics with your friends.
- It's okay to cut off contact when it's time to walk away. If

you tried and found that he or she was not to your particular liking, just quickly and politely end the conversation. You don't have to explain yourself, just be sure and do it with grace and without saying anything negative about him or her.

And, of course, there are some simple and obvious things you *should not* do when you're at the exposing stage of your new relationship:

- Don't brag about yourself.
- Don't talk about your long list of terrible ex's.
- Don't take or make a call on your cell phone.
- Don't check out other men or women.
- Don't dress or act provocatively or like a slob.
- Don't share *all* your information.
- Don't talk about sex.

A Final Note About Your Fig Leaves

Wearing fig leaves are a part of who we all have become over time. As we discussed, fear is as natural to us as breathing. But letting your fears control you doesn't have to be a part of who you are. If you need to work on those fig leaves, slow down and take some time to deal with them. Remember, you *destroy* your fig leaf by consciously doing the *opposite* of what it tells you to do. When it's difficult, just remember how your love substitutes have sabotaged your attempts at having relationships.

Dr. Ronn

Going Against Your Grain

Be bold enough to act contrary to your instincts! Be the first to call, instead of waiting for the other person to pick up the phone. Be the one who waits a little longer to see if the relationship is worth pursuing, instead of running away after the first conflict. Be the person who walks away the moment you know beyond a doubt that you're headed for a codependent relationship. Be the one who will take responsibility for the argument rather than blame the other person. Be the easy-going person who doesn't have to have every little thing "just right."

Stop trying to control all the factors that might injure your heart. Just as the blood flows through your veins, you *must* move forward every day. The finish line is where you meet Jesus face-to-face and you hope He says, "Well done, good and faithful servant."

It's not about all your acts of faith. It's not about how much money you make or how important you are. It's not even about who you love. It's all about *how* you love.

So love fearlessly! If you let fear stand in the way of opening your heart, then you're ignoring Jesus' greatest desire for you to "love one another. As I have loved you, so you must love one another" (John 13:34 NIV).

What's Next?

Facing your fears is definitely the turning point. But what you've learned so far won't amount to much or stay with you for long if you don't know how to balance your knowledge with your actions.

In the next chapter, you'll see how you can live a life full of love in partnership with another person without becoming consumed by it. Passion and desire are fires that burn with intensity, and even after marriage, it's easy to lose your personal identity. So take a little time to absorb everything you've learned thus far, and then join me in chapter nine.

Time to Make the Doughnuts

I have always loved pastries. Sugared, powdered, cinnamon-sprinkled, glazed, cream-filled, jelly-filled, baked, fried, and dipped in chocolate, I could eat doughnuts in place of three squares any day. Oh, and let's not forget the coffee—lots of cream and two sugars, please. And give me a shot of caramel in that.

I could eat sugary sweets every day, but that would wreak havoc on my waistline. Not to mention, Aladrian (bless her heart for taking such good care of me) would be all over my case about my health! So I abstain—most of the time. I had to learn to temper my sweet tooth with other good things like broccoli and cauliflower, whole grains, fruit, lots of water, and exercise. As I matured, it became easier for me to learn about balancing my health and sticking to a regimen.

It also got easier for me to balance other things in my life: finishing college; dating and eventually marrying Aladrian, the love of my life; having and raising our children with her; building a successful counseling practice; growing a God-directed church; writing books; traveling to and speaking at conferences around the world; and just hanging with my friends.

I actually remember the old days when I complained to my parents, "I'm bored!" But it seemed that each new year brought a new list of responsibilities and opportunities. Now there are times when I feel I can't take on one more thing. That's when I put the brakes on my life, evaluate where I spend my time, and determine what is most important—to me and to God. After all, I am only the steward of the gifts and time with which God blesses me.

Believe it or not, I figured out a lot about balance by observing a doughnut—the shape of it anyway. You're probably thinking, *All that sugar has made him silly.* But stay with me on this one, and I promise to teach you a valuable lesson about balancing your love life with your whole life.

9

Balance Your Love Life with Your Whole Life

It is good to grasp the one and not let go of the other.
The man who fears God will avoid all extremes.

ECCLESIASTES 7:18 NIV

✀

"Anita, how many times have we been through this now? Two? Three times?" Obviously I'm a little frustrated with Anita because I've counseled her through her last two (or three?) job changes. Each time it's the same old story. She starts dating a new guy (this time it's Charles), and pretty soon, she's spending all her time taking care of him, running all his errands, and ignoring her other obligations—even her own job. I haven't even seen her at church in over a month, and her mother called me last week and told me she hadn't heard from Anita in almost two weeks. The worst part is that she's been fired from yet another job because she fails to show up or calls in "sick" too often.

"I know! I'm just awful," pleads Anita. *"I swear I'm going to straighten up and fly right. It's just such a hectic time for Charles, and I want to help him as much as I can."*

"Maybe the best help you can give Charles is letting him take care of his own business. Maybe—and I'm just throwing this out there—the best help you can give yourself is to find this little thing called balance."

"Look, I know I have this problem. I just don't know what to do about it. I just can't have a relationship, work

full-time, take care of my mom's stuff, and spend time with my friends. There are not enough hours in the day!"

"Anita, there are plenty of hours in the day. God gave you twenty-four—just like everybody else. Now let's get to the bottom of this once and for all."

You're reading this book because you're seeking answers to important questions about love relationships. Up to this point, you've either laid low and kept out of the dating scene, or you've spent a little time out there testing the waters. The fact that you're still reading means you're ready to take your efforts to the next level. You're wise to understand that adding a relationship to your list of things to do is going to add something wonderful to your life, but at the same time, it's going to add a little stress and take some of your time.

My Doughnut Philosophy

I mentioned earlier that a great lesson about balance can be found in observing doughnuts, so let's get into it. My Doughnut Philosophy has two parts—the dough and the hole.

The "Dough" of the Doughnut

The dough of the doughnut is a circular con-figuration. Although your life definitely began at one point and will definitely end at another point, the unbroken circle of dough represents what your life is like *between* those two points. As the sun rises and sets day after day, you go through your daily routine—hopefully with a few adventures now and then. The adventures in life are the colorful sprinkles and sugar glaze on the doughnut.

Now look at this picture of the same doughnut separated into several different sections. Each section represents something in your life that takes time. The basic time consumption issues are home and family, school and career, solitude, leisure and hobbies, time with friends, love relationships, church, financial matters, and health. You may not have all these specific time consumptions, or you may have more than what I've noted here, but the point is this: Every one of these things takes time, and the more time you spend on one section, the less time you have for all the other sections. Every time you take a bite out of the doughnut, there is less doughnut!

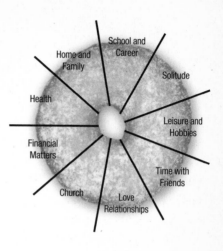

How Healthy Is Your Doughnut?

Spend some time thinking about how you apportion your doughnut—that is, your time and activities between home and family, work and school, friends, hobbies, church, love relationships, and so on. Do this and you'll see whether or not you have a balanced life. In fact, some of you may be sitting there dumbfounded because this is the *first* time you've noticed how unbalanced your life really is!

If it makes you feel any better, most people list their career as the biggest consumption of their time. Things like hobbies, solitude, and health usually give people the most pleasure, but those things often receive the least amount of their available time.

So how can you spend less time on the things that drain energy out of you and spend more time on the things that revitalize you?

Learn Time Management Principles. There are great books and magazines dedicated to helping you learn how to reorganize, prioritize, and manage your time. Here are a few excellent titles you should *make* time to read:

- *The Now Habit: A Strategic Program for Overcoming Procrastination and Enjoying Guilt-Free Play* by Neil Fiore[13]

- *A Minute of Margin: Restoring Balance to Busy Lives* by Richard A. Swenson
- *The One Minute Manager* by Kenneth H. Blanchard and Spencer Johnson
- *The Time Trap* by Alec MacKenzie
- *How to Get Control of Your Time and Your Life* by Alan Lakein
- *Time Tactics of Very Successful People* by B. Eugene Griessman

Get Help! It's okay to admit when you're overwhelmed, so get some help with the things you can't handle by yourself.

If you're stressed at work, talk to your boss about reassigning some of your most unproductive tasks, so you can devote more of your time to *more productive* things. A good supervisor will understand and appreciate your desire to be more productive. Try to spend less time in unproductive meetings, if possible. If you're not an essential member of a team effort, then see if you can skip the meeting and just get the minutes.

If your stress is at home and if you share your house with other people, make sure the household chores are split equally.

Unclutter Your Life. Something happens to the brain when a person walks into a cluttered room. The distraction level is higher and, therefore, focus is lower. Get rid of the junk in your office and at home. Clean off workspaces and put away nonessential items. Keep rooms clean by putting away items after you use them. Clean out your car. Clear all the old receipts and junk out of your wallet or purse. Have a yard sale once or twice a year to get rid of all the stuff piling up around the house and garage.

Once you unclutter your life, you'll find things faster, you'll remember where things are more easily, and you'll stop wasting time managing all your clutter—which is really managing *you!*

Slow Down. I know you're thinking, *Slow down? No way! I need to speed up! I don't have time to slow down!* But the truth is you don't have time to not slow down. Slowing your pace in life will give you a better focus on tasks at hand, and you can concentrate on doing things right the first time. Taking on tasks in a measured and methodical manner will allow you to complete them more efficiently and move on to the next thing without having to return to old tasks to redo them. Try it and you'll find that you're actually making time by taking time.

Get Physical. If you're in poor physical shape, you're going to have less energy, less stamina, and less enjoyment for all the tasks in your day. Try to get at least 30 minutes of exercise every day—even if it's just a brisk walk. Ideally you want to have good cardiovascular workouts mixed with core strength training two or three times a week. If at first you're not able to work out for that long, start slow and do what you can. Try taking a 15-minute walk every day this week. Work up to 30 minutes a day the following week, adding a little more time each week.

Put exercise on your calendar as a time-allotted task—you can get your exercise done each day without double-booking appointments. Exercising with a friend is a great way to increase both your Friends and Health sections.

Multitask. By doing similar activities together, you save a lot of time. For instance, manage your finances twice a month instead of every time you open your mail. At the same time, balance your checkbook. When you run to the bank, include errands to the post office and dry cleaners. Set aside the first hour of each workday to read all your e-mails *while* you're listening to the news on your computer. By doing this you can stop interrupting your day to respond to e-mails, and you don't have to take the time to read the news.

Here's a good tip: If you have e-mail notification turned on, turn it off. Those little windows that pop up on your computer screen encourage you to stop what you're doing and respond. Again, try writing and responding to your emails only once or twice a day during a designated time.

Do Less of What You Hate and Do More of What You Love. If you're terrible at managing your finances and spend long hours fighting to find 12 cents in your checking account, then hand your finances over to a bookkeeper. There are lots of reputable bookkeepers who will find your 12 cents in no time, and you can spend your time doing the things you love.

Likewise, if you hate cleaning, hire a cleaning agency to come in once a week. Send your laundry out to a cleaners. Drop your car at a detail shop. You might spend a little more money handing off the undesirable tasks, but it'll all balance out in your doughnut!

Give Yourself Permission to Play. You know what they say about all work and no play! It's okay to take time off and have a little fun—or even a lot of fun. Having fun and really enjoying yourself will make the rest of your life bearable, even in unbearable situations.

Take a vacation by yourself or with friends, go to a spa, buy a hammock, join a softball team, fly a kite, play with a yo-yo, get some bubble bath and take long soaks until you're wrinkly. Still looking for ideas? Go to a playground and watch little kids play. They've got it down to an art form.

Spend Time with God. Setting aside the first hour of your day to pray is a great way to start every day. You don't have to spend your prayer time asking God to give you the things you desire (although part of your prayer time may include that) or complaining about how hard your life is. Spend some time just praising and worshipping God for how great He is. Sing out loud and let Him know how thankful you are to have every second of the day He gives you.

By now you're following my Doughnut Philosophy and you can see that even if you don't eat doughnuts, they actually have some very practical lessons for life. The next time you pass a case of these delectable sugary delights, stop and muse over them a while. Think about managing your time and finding ways to do more of the things that make your heart come alive.

We're not finished with Doughnut Philosophy yet! There is one more element of the doughnut that's even more important than the dough.

The "Hole" of the Doughnut. If the part of the doughnut you eat is the part that consumes your time, and you determine how healthy your balance quotient is by the size of each section, then what is measured by the hole? The hole represents all the "inner" things of your life that give meaning to all the things on the outside. All the different areas that consume time are influenced by what's central to you. These are the deeper things—your calling or purpose in life, things resting in your soul that are uncompromised and immoveable, your self-image and self-esteem, how integrated your life is with others, the issues and causes you've decided to dedicate your life to, your emotional and spiritual health, your sensitivity and responsiveness to God, and all the elements of your outer life as a whole.

What Is This?

What this area looks like and how deep it is will determine how you allot your time to everything you do. Your goal should be simple: Be the same person in all places and all situations, no matter who is looking and no matter what you'll gain or lose. The way you do that is to make sure the center of your doughnut is a deep well of soulful things that sustain you from the inside out.

How Deep Is Your Well?

Now spend some time thinking about the importance you assign to the soulful things in your life—your calling or purpose, values, self-esteem, relationship with God, and so on. How easy or difficult is it to identify all the things that are central to you?

Dr. Ronn

The Comfortable Christian Life

I've come to believe that balance in the central, deeper area of my life will take care of everything that consumes my time simply because what is central to my soul reaches into all other areas.

This isn't a tightrope walk for me. Holding on to one and not letting go of the other doesn't mean I stand dead-center without moving. I'm constantly in motion, shifting and balancing things on the outside and on the inside. I'm adjusting my direction on a regular basis. But one thing is always clear to me: I know where I am at all times.

Don't think for a second that you'll be playing it safe by balancing your life. There will always be some give and take. That tension is necessary to help take your focus away from your need to control things or your desire to have a calm, stress-free, uncluttered, perfect life. If your life was perfect, you wouldn't need other people and you wouldn't need God.

The joy of having a balanced life only increases when you begin sharing it with another person. However, don't wait until you're in a relationship before you deal with your balance issues. Get into this step and work through finding your own Doughnut Philosophy (without eating too many of them).

Balancing Act

Don't let your love life become your whole life. Keep it balanced. Be sure you have a full life with lots of varied activities that challenge and thrill you. Frankly, it makes you a more interesting person—one worth getting to know!

Life is hard enough without having to carry the weight of your single life on your sleeve, so here are some simple guidelines for keeping it real in your love relationship while preserving your identity and having time for all the things you need and want to do:

- Don't spend every second with your love interest. There will be plenty of time for that when you're both advanced in years, sitting on the porch in your rocking chairs.

- Share friends—and have friends of your own. It's fun to do things as a couple with friends you have in common, but you need to have friends of your own that you can do things with in the absence of your love interest. This not only helps you keep a little of your personal identity, but it provides good conversation material when you meet up with your partner again.

- Share interests—and have some of your own. Again, it's fun to do things as a couple. The more you have in common, the easier it will be for the two of you to find things to do together. But you need to balance that time with hobbies and leisure activities that you can each do alone, those that give you plenty of joy and life.

- Relax and don't overanalyze or obsess about things. Everyone will have a lot more fun together if you're not trying to control or calculate every moment. Just let things happen and see where they take you.

What's Next?

Have you noticed that each chapter brings you a little closer to taking action? You're just about primed and ready to tackle dating—so let's keep moving.

All the planning and preparation in the world won't do you a lick of good if you don't put your plans into action, and action calls for making decisions. It's time for you to make a conscious effort to get out of your chair, get off the couch, get into a sharp-looking outfit, and get out the door. It's time to make some decisions!

CHAPTER TEN

It's a Jungle Out There

I used to love that old TV show *Wild Kingdom.* My favorite animals were the lions, and I remember being amazed that it was actually the lioness that went out and hunted down dinner for the family. I especially loved watching her hunt prey. It's amazing to see her so relaxed, so nonchalant. She looks so unaffected by her surroundings, so uninhibited by the fact that there are hungry cubs and a cranky man-cat at home. And yet we know what she's doing. She is using all her senses to locate a potential food source. She sneaks in as close as she can get to observe her prey, takes in the surroundings to gauge when and how she can best attack, and rests a moment before expending effort to bag the big meal. Calmly, she settles in the tall grass—watching and waiting.

Sometimes it's a short wait, sometimes it's a long wait. Regardless of how much time she spends in the tall grass, one thing is certain: She'll only succeed if she chooses to attack at the right moment.

Timing is everything, and it's not because she's afraid. It's because she's cautious. There's a lot riding on her success— and her failure.

The message is *not* that dating is like hunting for prey (although sometimes it feels like it), it's that making good decisions is a lot like being an experienced lioness on the hunt. Sometimes you'll have to make big decisions that will affect the rest of your life, perhaps even others' lives.

A lioness will not usually go after the biggest animal in the herd unless she has no other choice. Generally she'll go after the smaller animal. Most of our days are like that. Small decisions are necessary, less so for large ones.

The lioness's practice of waiting is a good lesson. We can follow her example by sitting calmly and quietly, gauging our surroundings, using our senses to test the environment, meditating on the correct course of action before leaping into success or failure.

But *timing* is everything. If the lioness attacks too soon, she can scare the herd, cause a stampede, and miss out on the prize. If she waits too long, she risks walking away empty-handed too.

There are solid and practical ways to make timely decisions that will help you on your way to *the one*. Romantic pursuits and love relationships are hard work, and because you're human, there will always be conflict. So join me in this last chapter and put yourself on the path to finding and keeping your soul mate.

10

Make Decisions

*And I pray this: that your love will keep on growing in
knowledge and every kind of discernment.*

PHILIPPIANS 1:9 HCSB

≈

*Todd started dating Cristin two weeks ago and already he's
thinking about the future. He's a nice young man, but he's
prone to making bad decisions.*

*"I just don't want to make the same mistakes I made
with Lisa," he says. "I dated her for almost an entire year
before I realized we weren't right for each other."*

"So what do you plan to do differently with Cristin?"

*"Well, for starters I'm not going to argue with her about
anything. Lisa and I argued about everything and look
where that landed us."*

"Do you really think you can avoid arguments?"

"Shouldn't we try to avoid arguments?"

*"The point is not to avoid conflict, Todd. The point is
to resolve conflict in a mutually respectful manner that will
bring growth to your relationship. Learning how to resolve
conflict is paramount to a successful relationship."*

*"But every decision Lisa and I tried to make led to a
fight."*

*"Well," I offered, "maybe your problem with Lisa was
not how you resolved conflict, but how you made decisions
that led to conflict."*

*"You're saying poor decision-making skills led to our
conflicts?" He is getting it. "You know, I have had conflicts*

at work too. They've even told me that I don't make deci-
sions well."

   "Todd, you have a lot of love inside you, and I applaud
you for thinking about your future with Cristin and not
wanting to repeat the mistakes you made with Lisa.
You're a bright young man, and I guarantee that you can
learn how to be a top-notch problem solver and decision
maker."

It seems appropriate to wrap up this final chapter with the same
Bible verse that opened the book. "And this I pray, that your love
may abound still more and more in knowledge and all discernment"
(Philippians 1:9). This verse is all about the power behind making
decisions—wise decisions made with the help of godly counsel, experience, and practice—and the desire to be a better person, a productive
member of society, and an asset to someone as a loving and mature
partner.

Everything you've read in the preceding chapters has been about
passive decision making. You've been studying, learning, waiting, and
sizing up your options. Now it's your turn to practice aggressive decision making, and you do it for these reasons:

- You want to learn how to be a wise, more mature decision
  maker.

- You want to avoid making costly and unnecessary mistakes
  just because you were impatient or acted too slowly.

- You know that it's your turn to act, and you have lots of
  options from which to choose.

In this final step, you'll make the decision to act. All the preparation
in the world won't get you anything unless you take action; so let's talk
about what you need to know about making decisions as you move
from passive to aggressive dating and recognizing your soul mate.

Decisions and the Phases of a Relationship

There are definite phases to every relationship. In each phase you will have decisions to make, conflicts to experience, and situations to face. You can read 20 different books with 20 different opinions about how many phases there are in a relationship. For the sake of simplicity, let's go with the common four-phase model and examine how each phase presents different challenges and how you can successfully navigate your way through them.

- Phase One: Getting to the first date
- Phase Two: Starting to know each other
- Phase Three: Sharing the deeper things
- Phase Four: Making an exclusive commitment

Phase One: Getting to the First Date

Reading this book has passively prepared you to aggressively take the initial step and get the first date with the person of your dreams. There are lots of decisions to be made at this stage and, fortunately, not a lot of conflict. The decisions are fairly simple ones:

- Do I want to go out with this person?
- Why do I want to date this person as opposed to someone else?
- Where should we go on our first date?
- What should I wear?
- What will we talk about?
- How much physical contact should there be?

As you see, the decisions are fairly superficial at this point. The less depth there is, the less potential for conflict. Thus there isn't much need for strong decision-making skills yet. You could almost make your decisions based on the outcome of a coin toss!

Phase Two: Starting to Know Each Other

After the first month or in the vicinity of three to four dates, you should know whether the person you're dating is worth further pursuit.

Dr. Neil Clark Warren, founder of eHarmony and author of several books about love and relationships, wrote a fantastic book called *How to Know if Someone is Worth Pursuing in Two Dates or Less.*[14] He certainly cuts to the chase! Some people can make the decision about whether they're with *the one* after just two dates, but most people need a little more time to uncover the "real" behind the relationship.

You've probably noticed that there's a lot of game playing going on out there—people wearing masks and hiding behind their fig leaves. Sometimes the old-fashioned way is the only way to cut through it all—just spending time with them. But the more time you spend with someone, the more likely you are to see something you may not like. At this point, there are questions that go a little deeper and an increased potential for superficial conflicts that require basic decision-making skills. Some of your issues may look like this:

- Will she expect me to continue spending that much money every time we go out?
- Will he keep talking about his old girlfriends?
- Will my parents like her?
- Will he like my friends?
- Will her differing religious upbringing become a problem?
- What does my future look like if I continue seeing this person?

Again, the more time you spend with someone, the more likely you are to discover differences that may cause conflict. At this stage in the relationship, you probably won't have any knock-down, drag-out fights. (If you are, that's a pretty good indication that you shouldn't be together!) However, you may have your first disagreement that will require problem-solving and decision-making skills.

For instance, ladies, if you've noticed during the first couple of dates that he likes to flirt with other girls, then this might be how your conversation will play out (first I'll give an example of two people making wise decisions):

The Wise Path

Laura: Laura makes a decision to mention her concerns about flirting to Kevin, her date, because this is an issue that is important to her. It may even be one of the things she simply cannot live with. Calmly, and away from anyone who could overhear, Laura says, "Kevin, the last two times we were out together, I've noticed that you talk to other girls in what seems to be a very flirtatious manner."

Kevin: He makes a decision about how he wants to respond. With true and genuine concern, Kevin says, "I'm sorry, Laura, I didn't even realize I was doing it. I have always had such an outgoing personality that I just thought I was being friendly."

Laura: Laura responds to Kevin's remarks and further explains her concern. Looking Kevin in the eye, Laura gently responds, "And I'm sorry for being so sensitive to it, but I've had a few bad experiences in the past with boyfriends cheating on me. I know you're an extroverted person, and I really like that about you, but this is something that is very important to me. I want to feel secure in my growing relationship with you. So can we agree that I'll be less sensitive and you'll be a little less friendly?"

Kevin: Kevin lets Laura know he understands her concern and responds as a man who respects her and wants her to be confident in their relationship. Looking Laura in the eye and placing a hand gently on hers, Kevin says, "I want to assure you that I'm not the unfaithful type, but you'll have to learn that about me over time. I respect you and I'm sorry you had those bad experiences. I'm going to do everything I can to moderate my friendliness. Please don't be afraid to let me know in the future if you think I'm being inconsiderate in this way."

Now, I know we all wish that every conflict could be that civil and calm. Sometimes it's not. Here is an example of that type of conflict:

The Foolish Path

Laura: Laura makes a decision to mention her concerns about flirting to Kevin, her date, because this is an issue that is important to her. It may even be one of the things she simply cannot live with. Loudly and in front of everyone in the restaurant, Laura says, "Kevin, you always flirt with other women when we're out together. Knock it off or we're through."

Kevin: He makes a decision about how he wants to respond. Kevin says, "Check, please!"

You see? Kevin and Laura came to a crossroad early in their relationship, and because they both lacked the maturity and ability to make wise decisions, their crossroad turned into a dead end.

When you're spending time getting to know someone, it's important to remember everything you learned in chapters four and five about how you package yourself and in chapter seven about how to approach people and be approachable yourself. If your new relationship seems like it has potential, you don't want to blow it by exposing the wrong package or approaching it like a derailed freight train.

A simple rule of thumb at this stage of a relationship is to weigh your decisions against a ten-step criteria:

1. Decide if there really is a problem.

2. Identify what the problem is and decide whether you want to try to solve it.

3. Before you approach the conflict, look at other courses of action you could take (based on your values) and what goals would be accomplished by taking each of those courses.

4. Clearly define the criteria for your opinions.

5. Choose a course of action only after considering all possibilities.

6. Don't make assumptions about people or situations.

7. Don't make any decisions based on the strong emotions of either party.

8. Listen to what the other person is saying.

9. Reach an agreement or continue to civilly debate until the matter is settled.

10. When it's clearly settled, leave it in the past.

Also, don't forget the benefit of wise counsel. There are many people who can offer you the benefit of their wisdom and experiences. Take advantage of any free advice that's offered in love and respect for what you're facing.

Phase Three: Sharing the Deeper Things

Between the third and sixth month, you should be able to decide whether or not the person you're dating is someone with whom you want to discuss a future together.

Moderate conflicts are common at this stage and the questions you ask yourself can change the course of your future. Therefore, mature decision-making abilities are vital, and you should receive counseling from your pastor or close, mature friends to help you through the tough times. Some common questions you can ask yourself at this stage may include:

- Would he or she make a good spouse?
- Would he or she make a good parent to our children?
- How does he or she manage personal finances?
- How would we handle joint finances?
- What are his or her views about sex and will he or she respect my views?
- Can I share very confidential parts of my life with him or her?
- Will he or she respect my space and privacy, even though we're spending a lot more time together?

There are two typical obstacles to building the relationship and resolving conflict at this stage. First, because you've already devoted so much time to the relationship, you're likely to suffer from sketchy thinking and delays in making the tough decisions. You might think, *I've put five months into this—do I want to throw that away?* The answer is apparent when you determine how important this issue is. Go back to your lists from chapter three and look at the things you said you could live with and the things you couldn't live without. You might think, *Maybe the problem will just go away.* But problems don't just go away—you have to work them out and find resolution.

The second obstacle arises because you know so much more about each other. Sometimes the things you learn are very deep and personal. By now you know exactly where to stick the knife—and you're learning just how deep you can stick it before it hurts. The sad truth is that humans can be very petty and hurtful at times. If backed into a corner, we can turn into some pretty ugly creatures.

Let's look at this disagreement between Brad and Carol and the decisions they made that could have damaged their relationship.

"Carol, we're going to my brother's for Thanksgiving, and that's final. No one in my family has met you yet, so I want

you to wear that blue outfit I like—and the diamond neck-
lace I bought you. And don't say anything to them about
me not getting that promotion."

"First of all, Brad, I haven't decided where I am going for
Thanksgiving. Second of all, I don't like the way you tell me
what to wear! You act as if I'm your trophy or something.
And stop telling me what to say in front of people. I'm not
an idiot."

This is the turning point in this discussion, where a decision is made
to either remedy an out-of-control situation or make it worse.

"Oh...sorry, Carol. I just assumed that we'd go to my
brother's because we're going to your parents' house for
Christmas. And you're right, you can wear whatever you
want. Honestly, I don't think you're an idiot. In fact, I think
you're brilliant. I'm just nervous about going to my brother's
house. He's always been so much better than me at everything, and well frankly, I always feel a little inadequate when
I'm with him."

Carol has a choice, too, at this point. She can say:

"Yeah? Well, it's not my fault your brother is better than
you. Maybe you should work harder and spend less time
playing golf and trying to impress people. You might have
even been able to buy me a bigger diamond."

That response would land the relationship in the trash heap. But
what if Carol said:

"Brad, I don't even know why I bit your head off like that,
except that I'm just really sensitive to being bossed around.

I'm sorry for being overly sensitive. I know you *feel* inadequate compared to your brother, but you're not. You have
wonderful and unique qualities that I love, and I respect
the man that you are."

Again, weigh your decisions against the ten-step criteria illustrated
in phase two. It's the only way to make decisions you can live with—
even if you make a mistake.

One more thing about this stage of the relationship concerns the
love and sex issue. Don't be fooled into thinking that love and sex are
interchangeable and that they are the *only* issues to address in your
future relationship. Moving too quickly into decisions about sex will
take your relationship in a direction you do not want to go just yet.
Trust me on this!

It takes time for two people to knit their souls together. Basing your
relationship on sex that you *think* is love will eventually bring your
relationship to a screeching halt when you realize that there are other
more vital aspects to cultivate. Sex isn't everything, and at this stage
of your relationship, it shouldn't even be a topic to explore beyond a
general discussion.

Phase Four: Making an Exclusive Commitment

Between the sixth and ninth month of dating, two people should
be ready to say, "Okay, we've been doing this long enough to know
that we're good together. It's time to take the next step and define our
relationship in exclusive terms."

For people who have been dating, waiting, and searching for their
soul mate, this is the stage when they may hear angels singing, "It's
really happened! You've found *the one!*" But there are still conflicts that
can occur—maybe more now than ever—and there are still decisions
to be made. You see, the longer you know someone, the more you see
their flaws, the more you experience the pain of disappointment, and
the more you come to realize that this person you're in love with is just

so…human. Humans have a great capacity for love, but we also have a great capacity for inflicting pain on one another. This stage of the relationship can bring out our ugly parts if we're not mature enough to handle a long-term relationship. Being open to your feelings and not being afraid to ask the tough questions are important. Some of your questions at this stage may look like this:

- Should we talk about getting engaged? When?
- How long should we be engaged before we get married?
- How will sex play into our relationship? Since I'm still planning to wait until marriage, will you respect that?
- What about our living situation? If we get married, where will we live?
- Do I need to start planning to relocate or change my career?

As you can see, the questions get more intense and the decision-making abilities you'll need at this stage will have to be mature and seasoned. You would be very wise to consult with people who have life experiences beyond your own. Do your homework! Don't get stuck in a bad situation that will cause you to look back later and think, *I should have seen this coming.*

Remember, these four relationship phases are not chiseled into stone. You shouldn't expect your current relationship to advance through the phases at the same pace as your last relationship. It may take two years to get to phase four. Everyone is different, and you should respect your partner's pace, just as he or she should respect yours.

Reviewing Previous Decisions

It's very important not to rest on your laurels as the relationship progresses. You have to be ready and willing to review your decisions and adjust your plans and perceptions accordingly. Not all the choices you make at the beginning of a relationship will look the same six months down the road. And the decisions made at six months will look different at twelve months, and so forth.

After you get to know someone better, there may be some things you're willing to compromise on. On the other hand, there may be things that were a little hazy in the beginning, and through the progression of the relationship, you decided they were deal-breakers for you.

Don't be afraid to make the tough decisions—even if you've put a lot of time into the relationship. The temporary discomfort you might feel after making that tough decision cannot compare to a life of misery that can't be fixed.

Change Happens

Being able to specifically dictate what kind of partner you want is probably the best part of having some degree of decision-making control in the action stage. The downside is that the more specific you get, the more you narrow your pool of prospective partners. Thank goodness you're only looking for one.

Defining your parameters makes sure *the one* is the kind of one you were looking for all along. It's good to know you can get as close to the desire of your heart as possible because you clarified what you wanted early on.

A great marriage is not when the "perfect couple" comes together. It is when an imperfect couple learns to enjoy their differences.

DAVE MEURER

The definition of parameters is too important to kick to the curb once you've started the dating process. You've got to keep defining and redefining because things change—and you have to change with them. So every week or every month, go back and revisit your lists and make adjustments as needed. This is a good time to realize that he or she does not have to be perfect to be perfect.

Redefining says you're not willing to let a relationship go forward once you see that person is not the kind you're looking for. Redefining also means you're not willing to waste another minute of your time investing in people who are not in your target market.

Finally, the Decision *Not* to Date

The final aspect of having decision-making control over your dating life is deciding *not* to have one. If you forget everything else you've read in this book, remember one thing: You don't have half a life as a single person. You see, God doesn't just start blessing your life after you get married. Your singleness is not some kind of defect or dysfunction that we need to lay hands on for healing.

This book was not meant to preach to you single folks about how to get married. God's purpose for your life is that you have a *whole life,* no matter if you're single, dating, or married. What you take away from this book will help you make wise decisions about dating, but it will also help you make wise decisions about staying single, if that's what you choose to do.

For some of you, marriage won't be the end of your story. Some of you may not make it to the altar. Does that mean the pursuit of love is a waste of your time? What if God stopped pursuing you and you stopped pursuing Him? Never forget that love is a very big deal to God. He constantly talks about love and the provisions He made to love you—and He constantly demonstrates that love.

If you spend the rest of your life working faithfully toward every kind of love relationship possible, and at the end of your story God says, "Well done, my good and faithful servant—you were faithful over that little bit, now let Me show you what love really looks like," then, believe me, you won't complain. The pursuit is definitely worth it whether you end your life single or married.

What Do You Do Now?

You've diligently worked your way through this book, read all the chapters, and thought long and hard about it. No doubt your mind is chock-full of thoughts, prayers, dreams, and plans. Now is the time to translate plans into action.

As you close this book and put your plan into action, I want to leave you with a final word of encouragement.

A Final Word

Congratulations! You've made it to "The End" (which is really "The Beginning"). Together we've examined your dating style to determine what's working and what's not and how to maximize your assets and minimize your liabilities. Whatever your particular situation is, I believe this book came into your possession for a significant purpose: positive change that will dramatically upgrade the quality of your love life now and far into the future.

After nearly two decades as a relationship therapist, self-help author, and minister of the Gospel, I'm convinced that those who find their soul mates and experience a serious, deeply satisfying relationship aren't necessarily more attractive, smarter, or more treasured by God than those who never do. The difference is the intentional decision to prepare themselves for love—and to boldly participate in the process. The bottom line: Those who do nothing usually go nowhere. But those who are willing to prepare and participate massively increase their potential for relationship success. Which kind are you?

Everybody likes to *hear* about opportunities to improve their lives—especially their love lives. Sadly, most people never commit themselves to seizing those opportunities. Instead they focus on all the reasons not to, such as lack of time, fear of failure, the inconvenience of it all, and that endless list of "what ifs." So once again they end up doing the same old thing—nothing. And when you do the same old thing over and over, you usually get the same old results—nothing.

My hope is that you're ready to do something new in order to gain something new and improved in your love life. You know, you really *can* rise above the inevitable challenges and make ready for your *just-right* relationship—one that's richer than you ever could have imagined.

Sure, upgrading your confidence, your clarity and your dating savvy can take time. I suspect you'll be fine-tuning some of the skills you've been introduced to here far into the future. Neither you nor I can predict exactly where all the momentum you've gained is headed. Maybe your soul mate is just around the corner. Maybe not. Maybe marriage is in your future. It's certainly possible, but not guaranteed. We do know this much: *If you wait for perfect conditions, you will never get anything done...* (Ecclesiastes 11:4 TLB).

Now is not the time to wait, but to take bold action. Go back through this book reflecting on the specific bits of advice that have the most personal relevance for you. Make a list of them and then number the items in order of priority to work on. Commit to diligently work on no more than three at a time until you become strong in them. Then move to another set of three. Set your pace, keep your focus, and above all, let yourself be very proud of your demonstrated commitment to living what you've learned here.

It has taken this relationship coach 200 pages to bring you the very best of my insight and inspiration for your love life. But I'll leave the last words to the Master Relationship Coach, the One who completely knows who and how you are and what every detail of your future looks like. Even if you forget the words I've shared with you here, I encourage you to never forget His: *Make a careful exploration of who you are and the work you have been given, and then sink yourself into that...[Do] the creative best you can with your own life. At the right time we will harvest a good crop if we don't give up, or quit* (Galatians 6:4-5,9 MSG).

Dr. Ronn Elmore

Notes

1. Michael, Robert T., et al., *Sex in America: A Definitive Survey* (New York: Little, Brown & Company, first edition, 1994).

2. U.S. Census Bureau, American Fact Finder, OT-P18, *Marital Status by Sex, Unmarried-Partner Households, and Grandparents as Caregivers: 2000,* Data Set: Census 2000 Summary File 3 (SF 3)—Sample Data, Geographic Area: United States, http://factfinder.census.gov/servlet/ QTTable?_bm=y&-geo_id=01000US&-qr_name=DEC_2000_SF3_U_QTP18&-ds_name=DEC_2000_SF3_U (accessed 3/28/07). These statistics refer to people that have never married, widowed, or divorced. 41.4 percent (or 44,335,566) are men while 45.4 percent (or 51,812,612) are women.

3. TopDatingTips.com, *Dating Statistics: Top Dating Tips Poll Statistics,* http://www.topdatingtips.com/dating-statistics.htm (accessed 3/13/07).

4. MisterPoll, *What Do Men Find Most Attractive About Women,* http://www.misterpoll.com/results.mpl?id=2405574205 (accessed 3/12/07). MisterPoll also report 20 percent of respondents that say personality is most important, whereas 7 percent say looks are most important.

5. *National Geographic* magazine, "Singles," February 2007, http://bp3.blogger.com/_vd1k5R2x_ms/RbA8FjmbUEI/AAAAAAAAADg/wP6jftoYPzc/s1600-h/ng_singles.jpg (accessed 3/18/07).

6. Ibid. This chart also shows the largest concentration of single women in the New York, Newark, New Jersey, Connecticut area. There are reportedly 185,000 more single women than men in this location.

7. Three excellent resources on the Holy Trinity are available through the publishers: Letham, Robert, *The Holy Trinity: In Scripture, History, Theology and Worship,* (Phillipsburg, NJ: P&R Publishing, 2005). Benson, Clarence, *The One True God: Father, Son, and Holy Spirit* (Biblical Essentials Series) (Wheaton, IL: Crossway Books, 2004). George, Timothy, *God the Holy Trinity:*

Reflections on Christian Faith and Practice (Beeson Divinity Studies) (Grand Rapids: Baker Academic, 2006).

8. Eggerichs, Emerson, *Love and Respect* (Nashville: Thomas Nelson, 2004).

9. Eldredge, John, *Wild at Heart* (Nashville: Thomas Nelson, 2001).

10. You can find out more about managing your money and sign up for Dave Ramsey's Financial Peace University in your area by visiting their Web site: http://www.daveramsey.com/fpu/home/.

11. Crabb, Larry, et al., *The Silence of Adam: Becoming Men of Courage in a World of Chaos* (Grand Rapids: Zondervan, 1995).

12. Cloud, Henry, and John Townsend, *Boundaries: When to Say YES, When to Say NO, to Take Control of Your Life* (Grand Rapids: Zondervan, 1992).

13. Fiore, Neil, *The Now Habit: A Strategic Program for Overcoming Procrastination and Enjoying Guilt-Free Play* (New York: Tarcher, 2007). Swenson, Richard A., *A Minute of Margin: Restoring Balance to Busy Lives* (Colorado Springs: NavPress, 2003). Blanchard, Kenneth H., and Spencer Johnson, *The One Minute Manager* (New York: HarperCollins Business, 2000). MacKenzie, Alec, *The Time Trap* (Washington, DC: American Management Association, 1997). Lakein, Alan, *How to Get Control of Your Time and Your Life* (New York: Signet Books, 1996). Griessman, B. Eugene, *Time Tactics of Very Successful People* (New York: McGraw-Hill, 1994).

14. Warren, Neil Clark, *How to Know If Someone Is Worth Pursuing in Two Dates or Less* (Nashville: Thomas Nelson, 2005).

About Dr. Ronn Elmore

Ronn Elmore, Psy.D., is a noted Christian counselor and bestselling author. He has more than 20 years experience counseling marriage-minded singles and dating couples in a thriving Los Angeles-based practice. Elmore is a sought-after speaker, guest for television and radio shows, and a contributing writer for *Essence, Gospel Today,* and other publications and Web sites.

No-Nonsense Dating was inspired by the many men and women around the country who have experienced powerful transformations in their relationships after attending Dr. Ronn's high-impact seminars.

Dr. Ronn is available for conferences, seminars, and other speaking engagements, inspiring his audiences on topics related to interpersonal relationships—marriage, dating, parenting/family life, and personal performance.

The Ronn Elmore Group, Ltd.
5050 Laguna Blvd. Suite 112
Elk Grove, Ca 95758
Phone: (916) 760-0401
e-mail: Info@DrRonn.com

For additional relationship-enhancing resources visit
www.DrRonn.com

*More excellent books on relationships
from Harvest House Publishers*

ENDING THE SEARCH FOR MR. RIGHT: HOW TO BE FOUND BY THE MAN YOU'VE BEEN LOOKING FOR

Michelle McKinney Hammond

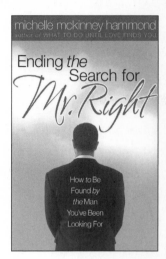

Does the journey toward finding a mate for life have to be filled with anxiety, desperation, fret, or regret? Not according to bestselling author Michelle McKinney Hammond who expertly navigates the choppy waters of singledom—for both men and women. She warmly encourages those stuck in the dead-end dating scene as well as those on an involuntary relationship fast that marriage could be on the horizon.

With her tell-it-like-it-is style using biblical examples, Michelle urges you to place your need for love in perspective, take life off hold, live purposefully, and gain a basic understanding of successful relating with the opposite sex.

This unique format is presented for both sides of the single coin. Women will welcome Michelle's sisterly advice and men will appreciate the insider information. Together, they comprise the ultimate guide to successfully finding (and keeping) the love of your life.

SINGLES AND RELATIONSHIPS

Dick Purnell and Kris Swiatocho

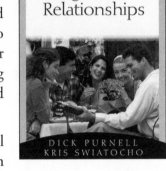

More adults than ever before are remaining single. And many of these unattached men and women are Christians who wonder if God will ever bring a mate their way…or if they should just stop focusing on a future with a marriage partner and live their single life to the fullest.

During a month-long study, you will learn how to cultivate friendships in general…and also with potential mates. In addition, you will discover how to deepen your most important intimate friendship—your relationship with your heavenly Father.

DATING WITH PURE PASSION: MORE THAN RULES, MORE THAN COURTSHIP, MORE THAN A FORMULA

Rob Eagar

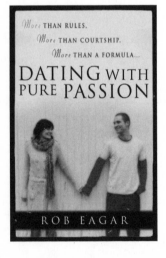

For Christian singles, spiritual union with Christ must be the foundation of all of their relationships—including dating relationships. Rather than looking to people to meet needs only God can fulfill, you will learn how to let Christ's sacrificial love ignite a passionate desire to share His love with a special person.

Each chapter concludes with a personal Bible study as well as group discussion questions, making this a valuable resource for private devotions, small groups, or premarital counseling.

To learn more about Harvest House books
or to read sample chapters, log on to our Web site:

www.harvesthousepublishers.com

HARVEST HOUSE PUBLISHERS

EUGENE, OREGON